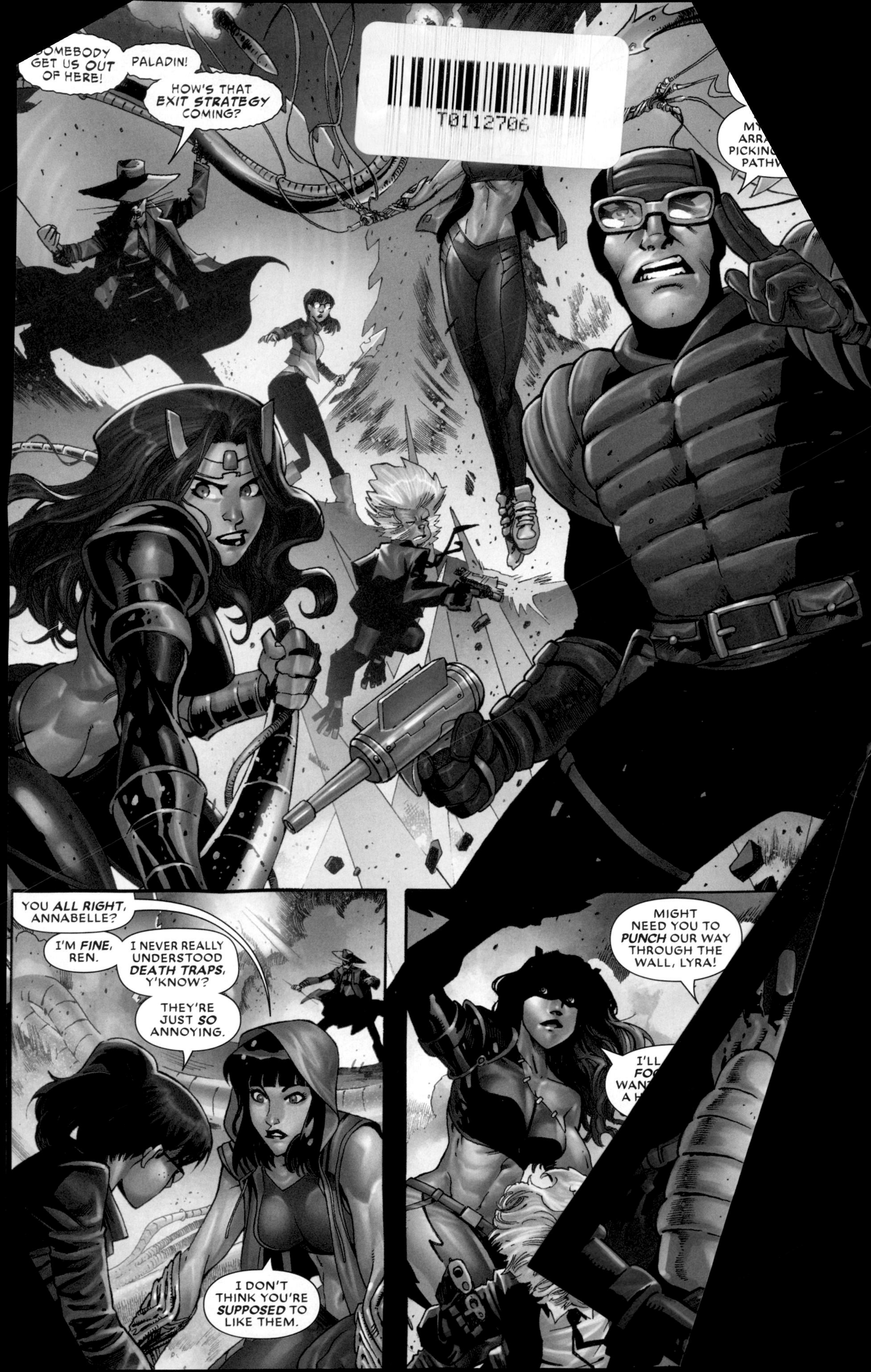

SOMEBODY GET US OUT OF HERE!
PALADIN!
HOW'S THAT EXIT STRATEGY COMING?
YOU ALL RIGHT, ANNABELLE?
I'M FINE, REN.
I NEVER REALLY UNDERSTOOD DEATH TRAPS, Y'KNOW?
THEY'RE JUST SO ANNOYING.
I DON'T THINK YOU'RE SUPPOSED TO LIKE THEM.
MIGHT NEED YOU TO PUNCH OUR WAY THROUGH THE WALL, LYRA!

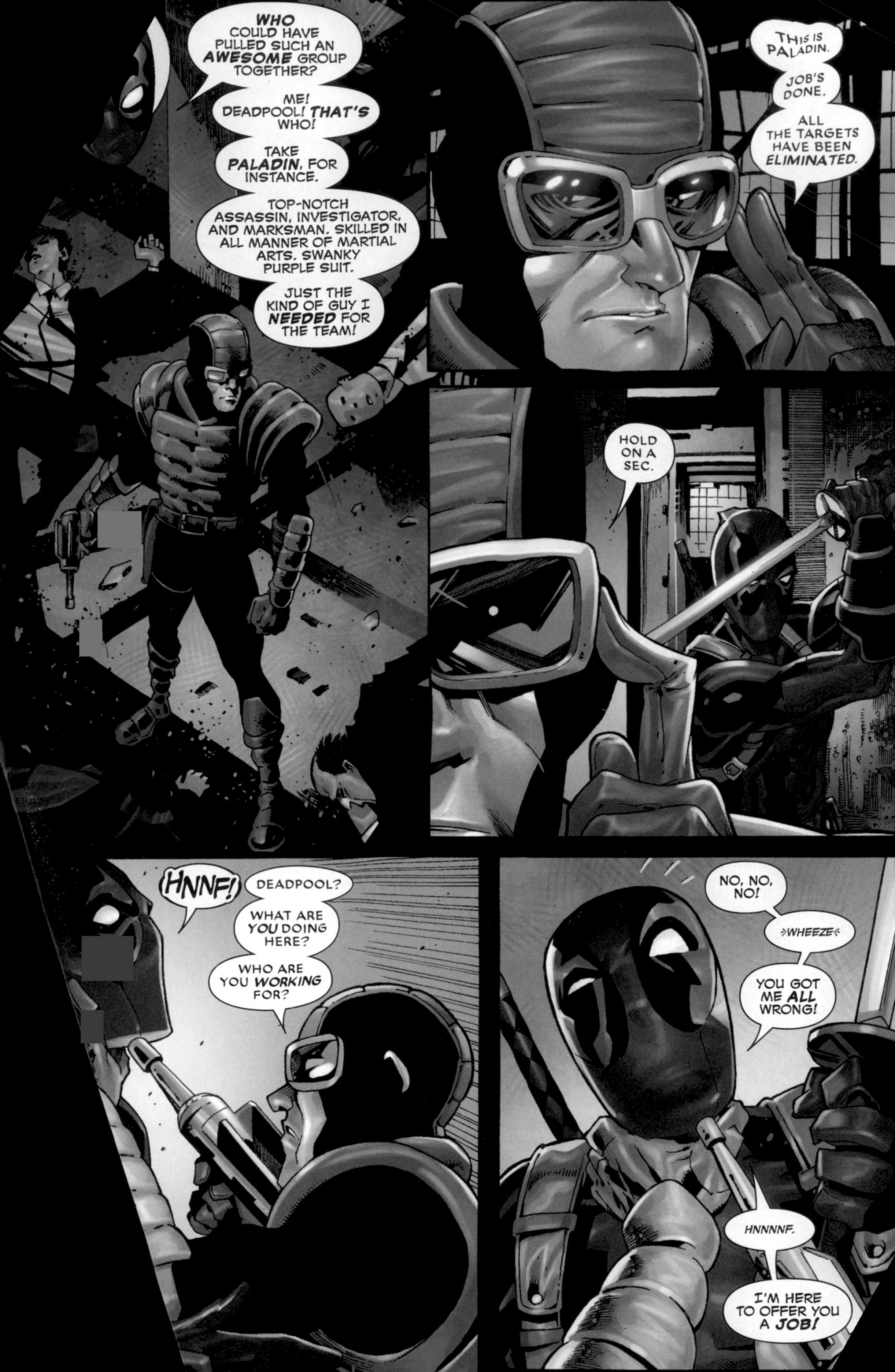
WHO COULD HAVE PULLED SUCH AN AWESOME GROUP TOGETHER?
ME! DEADPOOL! THAT'S WHO!
TAKE PALADIN, FOR INSTANCE.
TOP-NOTCH ASSASSIN, INVESTIGATOR, AND MARKSMAN. SKILLED IN ALL MANNER OF MARTIAL ARTS. SWANKY PURPLE SUIT.
JUST THE KIND OF GUY I NEEDED FOR THE TEAM!
THIS IS PALADIN.
JOB'S DONE.
ALL THE TARGETS HAVE BEEN ELIMINATED.
HOLD ON A SEC.
HNNF!
DEADPOOL?
WHAT ARE YOU DOING HERE?
WHO ARE YOU WORKING FOR?
NO, NO, NO!
WHEEZE
YOU GOT ME ALL WRONG!
HNNNNF.
I'M HERE TO OFFER YOU A JOB!

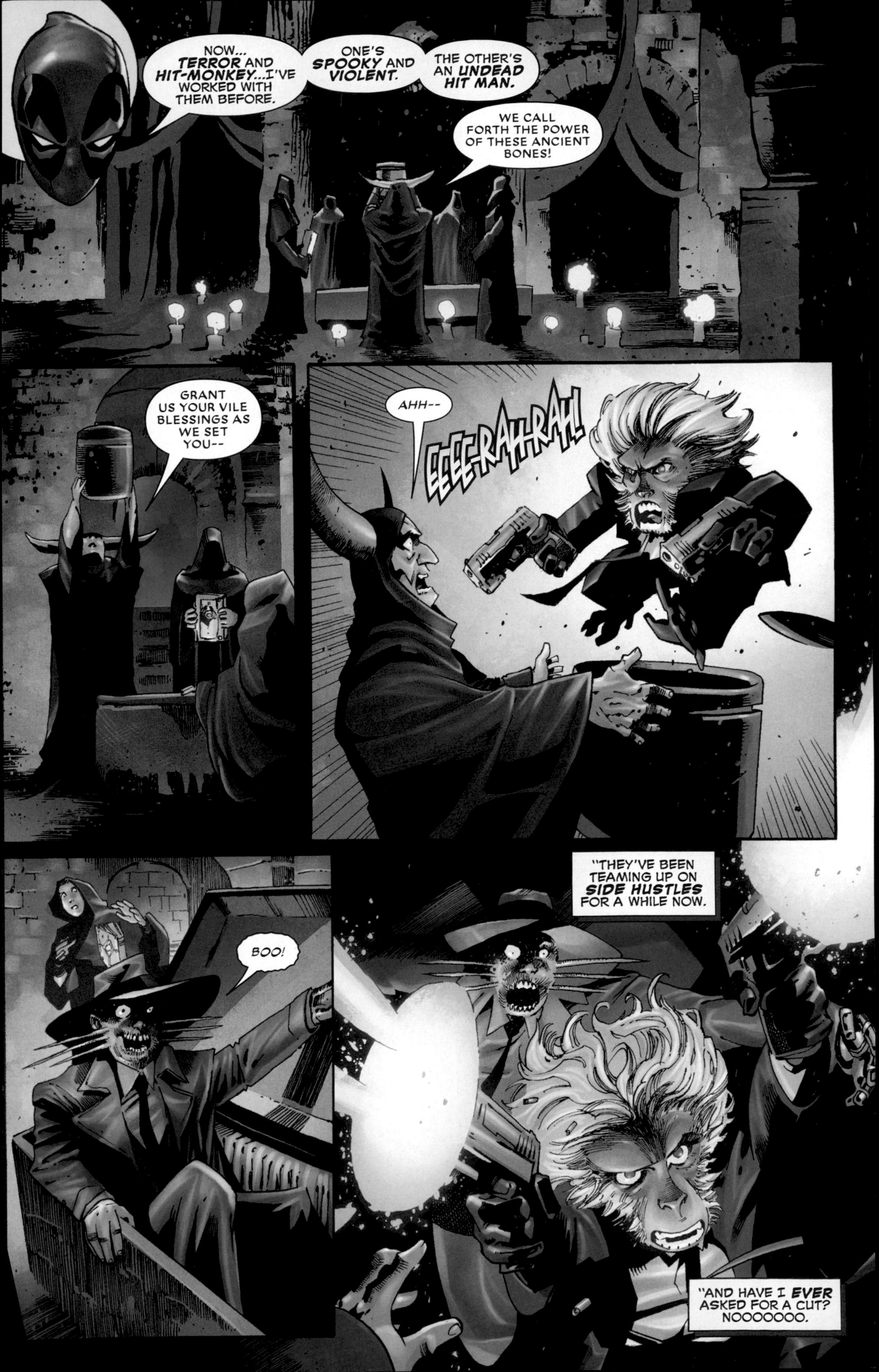

NOW... TERROR AND HIT-MONKEY...I'VE WORKED WITH THEM BEFORE.
ONE'S SPOOKY AND VIOLENT.
THE OTHER'S AN UNDEAD HIT MAN.
WE CALL FORTH THE POWER OF THESE ANCIENT BONES!
GRANT US YOUR VILE BLESSINGS AS WE SET YOU--
AHH--
EEEE-RAH-RAH!
BOO!
"THEY'VE BEEN TEAMING UP ON SIDE HUSTLES FOR A WHILE NOW.
"AND HAVE I EVER ASKED FOR A CUT? NOOOOOOO.

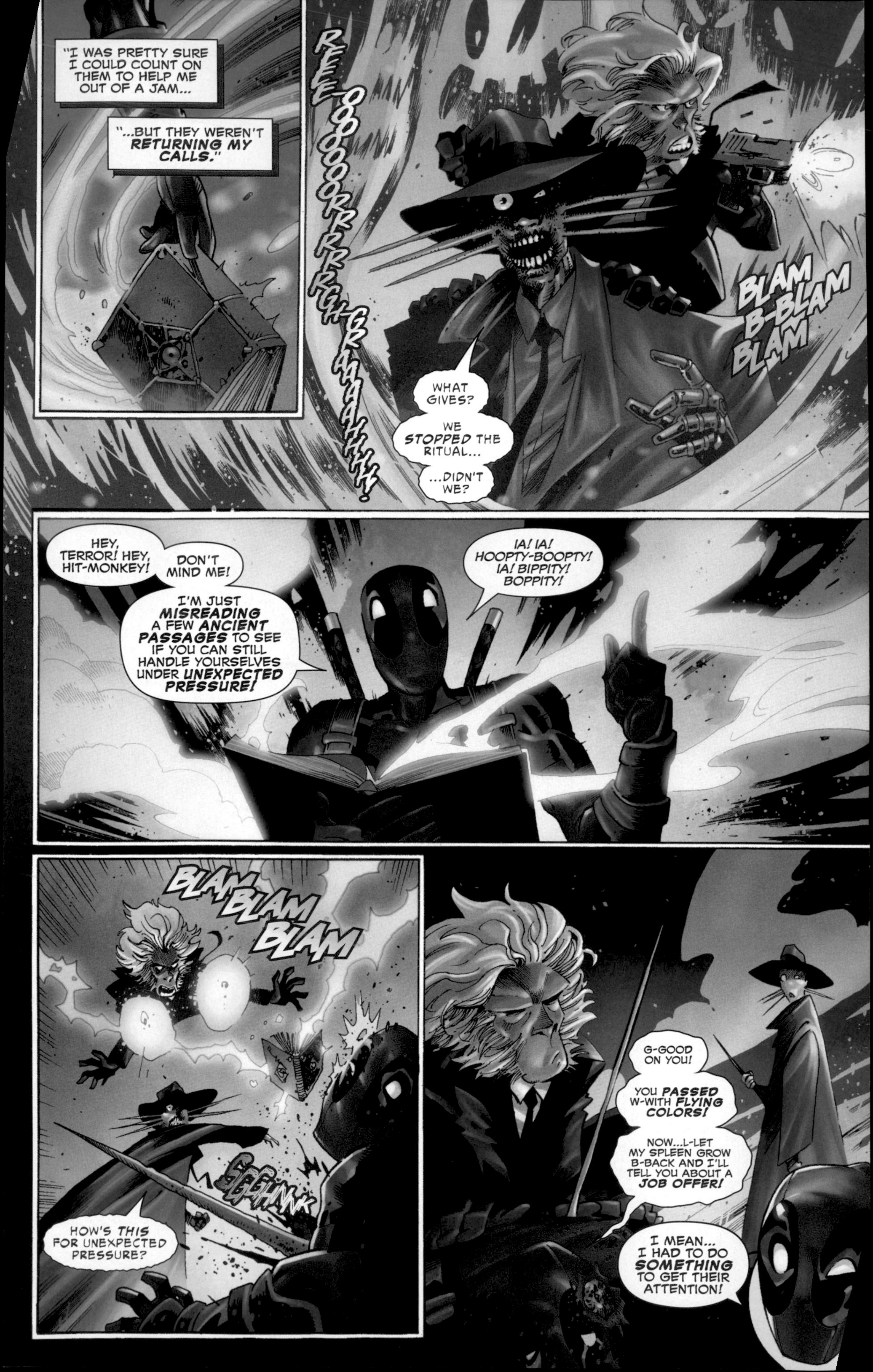

"I WAS PRETTY SURE I COULD COUNT ON THEM TO HELP ME OUT OF A JAM...
"...BUT THEY WEREN'T RETURNING MY CALLS."
REEE-OOOOOORRRRRGH-GRAAAAAHHH!
BLAM B-BLAM BLAM
WHAT GIVES?
WE STOPPED THE RITUAL...
...DIDN'T WE?
HEY, TERROR! HEY, HIT-MONKEY!
DON'T MIND ME!
I'M JUST MISREADING A FEW ANCIENT PASSAGES TO SEE IF YOU CAN STILL HANDLE YOURSELVES UNDER UNEXPECTED PRESSURE!
IA! IA! HOOPTY-BOOPTY! IA! BIPPITY! BOPPITY!
BLAM BLAM BLAM
SGGHNNK
HOW'S THIS FOR UNEXPECTED PRESSURE?
G-GOOD ON YOU!
YOU PASSED W-WITH FLYING COLORS!
NOW...L-LET MY SPLEEN GROW B-BACK AND I'LL TELL YOU ABOUT A JOB OFFER!
I MEAN... I HAD TO DO SOMETHING TO GET THEIR ATTENTION!

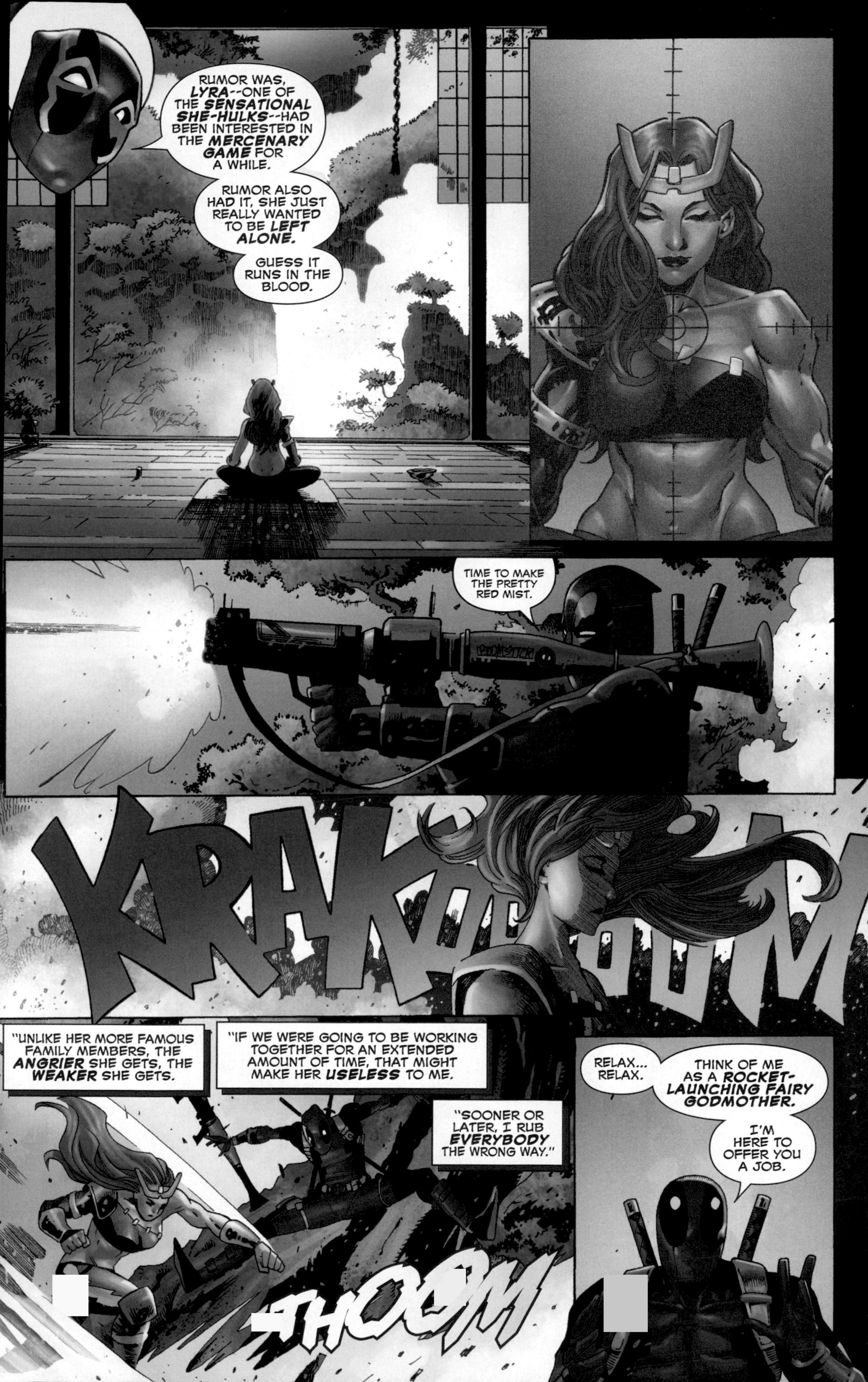
RUMOR WAS, LYRA--ONE OF THE SENSATIONAL SHE-HULKS--HAD BEEN INTERESTED IN THE MERCENARY GAME FOR A WHILE.
RUMOR ALSO HAD IT, SHE JUST REALLY WANTED TO BE LEFT ALONE.
GUESS IT RUNS IN THE BLOOD.
TIME TO MAKE THE PRETTY RED MIST.
KRAKOOOOM
"UNLIKE HER MORE FAMOUS FAMILY MEMBERS, THE ANGRIER SHE GETS, THE WEAKER SHE GETS.
"IF WE WERE GOING TO BE WORKING TOGETHER FOR AN EXTENDED AMOUNT OF TIME, THAT MIGHT MAKE HER USELESS TO ME.
"SOONER OR LATER, I RUB EVERYBODY THE WRONG WAY."
THOOM
RELAX... RELAX.
THINK OF ME AS A ROCKET-LAUNCHING FAIRY GODMOTHER.
I'M HERE TO OFFER YOU A JOB.

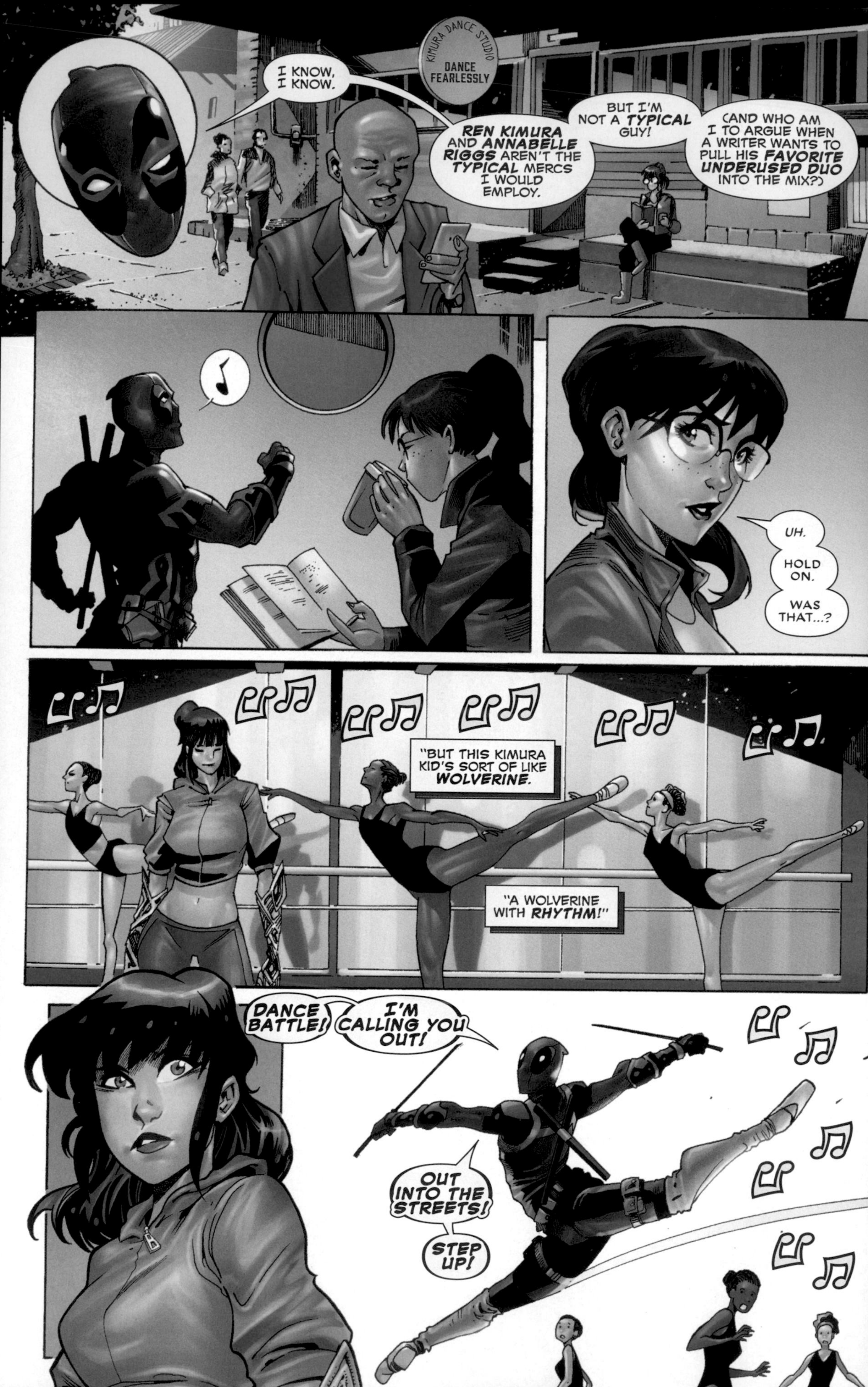

KIMURA DANCE STUDIO
DANCE FEARLESSLY
I KNOW, I KNOW.
REN KIMURA AND ANNABELLE RIGGS AREN'T THE TYPICAL MERCS I WOULD EMPLOY.
BUT I'M NOT A TYPICAL GUY!
(AND WHO AM I TO ARGUE WHEN A WRITER WANTS TO PULL HIS FAVORITE UNDERUSED DUO INTO THE MIX?)
UH.
HOLD ON.
WAS THAT...?
"BUT THIS KIMURA KID'S SORT OF LIKE WOLVERINE.
"A WOLVERINE WITH RHYTHM!"
DANCE BATTLE!
I'M CALLING YOU OUT!
OUT INTO THE STREETS!
STEP UP!

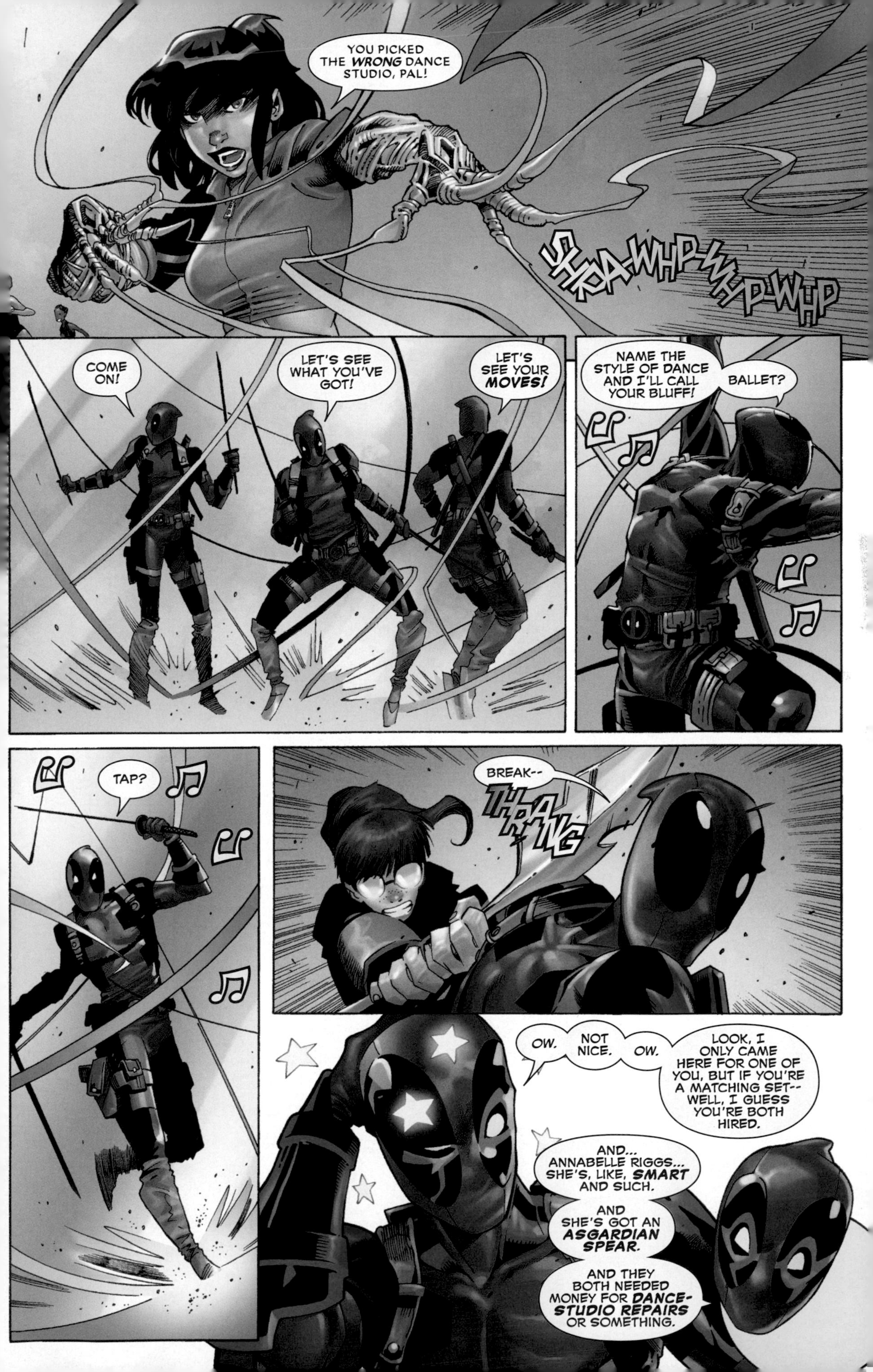
YOU PICKED THE WRONG DANCE STUDIO, PAL!
SHRA-WHP-WHP-WHP-WHP
COME ON!
LET'S SEE WHAT YOU'VE GOT!
LET'S SEE YOUR MOVES!
NAME THE STYLE OF DANCE AND I'LL CALL YOUR BLUFF!
BALLET?
TAP?
BREAK--
THRANG
OW.
NOT NICE.
OW.
LOOK, I ONLY CAME HERE FOR ONE OF YOU, BUT IF YOU'RE A MATCHING SET-- WELL, I GUESS YOU'RE BOTH HIRED.
AND... ANNABELLE RIGGS... SHE'S, LIKE, SMART AND SUCH.
AND SHE'S GOT AN ASGARDIAN SPEAR.
AND THEY BOTH NEEDED MONEY FOR DANCE-STUDIO REPAIRS OR SOMETHING.

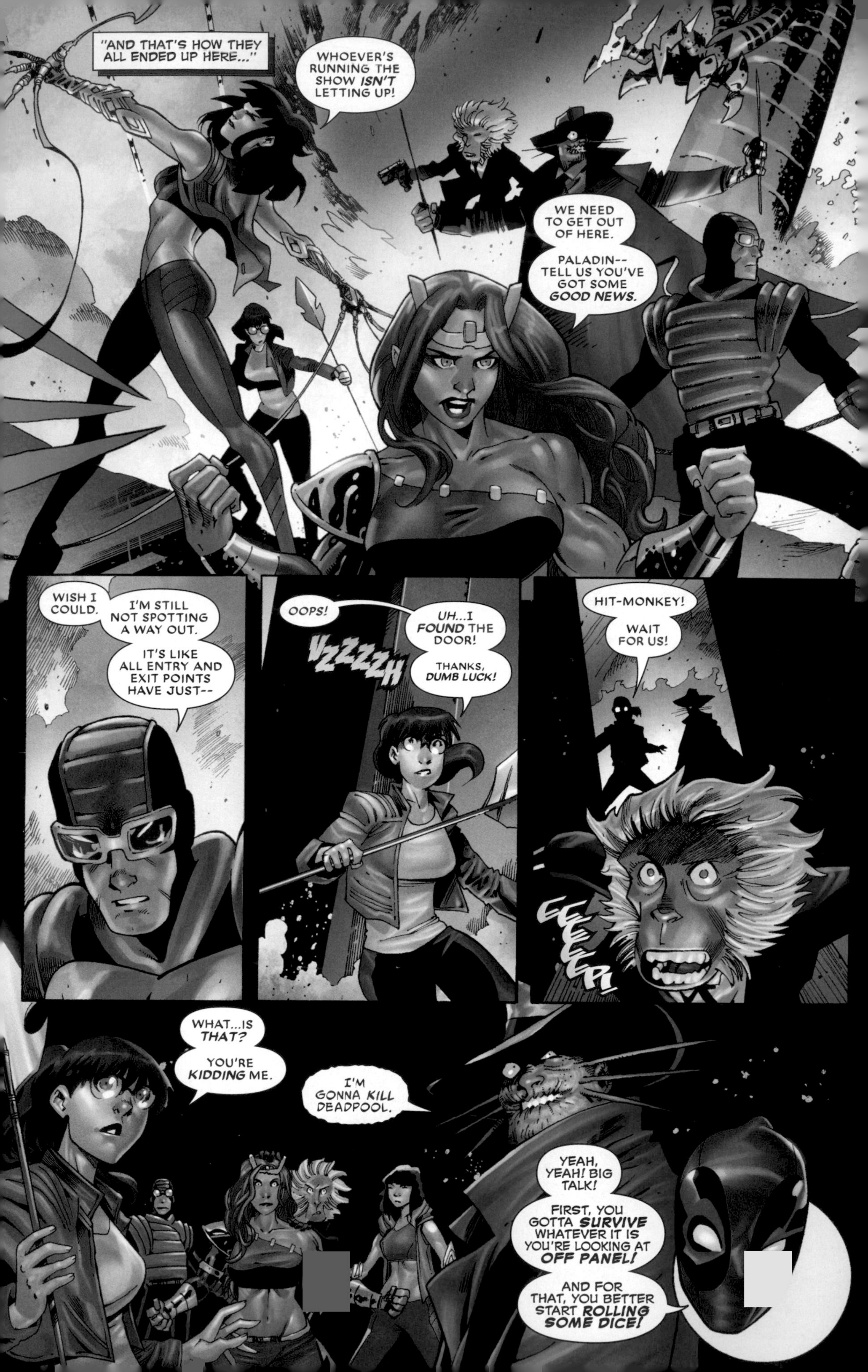
"AND THAT'S HOW THEY ALL ENDED UP HERE..."
WHOEVER'S RUNNING THE SHOW ISN'T LETTING UP!
WE NEED TO GET OUT OF HERE.
PALADIN-- TELL US YOU'VE GOT SOME GOOD NEWS.
WISH I COULD.
I'M STILL NOT SPOTTING A WAY OUT.
IT'S LIKE ALL ENTRY AND EXIT POINTS HAVE JUST--
OOPS!
VZZZZH
UH...I FOUND THE DOOR!
THANKS, DUMB LUCK!
HIT-MONKEY!
WAIT FOR US!
EEEEEP!
WHAT...IS THAT?
YOU'RE KIDDING ME.
I'M GONNA KILL DEADPOOL.
YEAH, YEAH! BIG TALK!
FIRST, YOU GOTTA SURVIVE WHATEVER IT IS YOU'RE LOOKING AT OFF PANEL!
AND FOR THAT, YOU BETTER START ROLLING SOME DICE!

/1/ LET'S GO!

WELCOME TO *DEADPOOL ROLE-PLAYS THE MARVEL Universe*. Break out your dice! Break out your character sheets! Break out the pizza and cheese puffs! Most of all, break out of your comfort zone and hurl yourself headlong into the rootinest-tootinest, rip-roaringest role-playing adventure in all of Marvel-dom!

In the story that awaits, the greatest hero who has ever existed recruits a band of unlikely mercenaries to embark on a wild adventure that takes them on a fantastic voyage to the far corners of the Marvel Universe. Along the way, those mercenaries (you know, the unlikely ones) encounter some of the strangest, toughest, coolest and most nefarious faces and heels in all of the comic-book universe.

Buckle up.

We're gonna wreck some stuff.

NARRATORS ONLY

First things first. If you're not the Narrator for this adventure, you need to stop reading right away! I know, I know. There are secrets ahead, and you, you dirty little secret peeper, want to see them. But if you deprive yourself of the thrill of discovery, you'll never forgive yourself. Years from now, when you're a broken shell of a human being, scraping your pennies together to afford therapy sessions to stop your psyche from crumbling like a wet knock-off brand sandwich cookie, you'll remember that time you read this book instead of experiencing it.

So…put it down. Don't turn the page.

Read the comic introduction a few more times. It's written by the best Deadpool writer in the biz. You know. Your favorite one. Then go no farther.

The monster at the end of the book is your own pathetic future.

Let the Narrator do the hard work while you do your level best to disrupt their plans and make them cry themself to sleep at night.

Or you can just go ahead and read it. Whatevs. Just understand that you'll be spoiling everyone's fun, worst of all your own. You'll be breaking the fourth wall, and people who do that are real jerks.

WHAT YOU NEED

You'll need the *Marvel Multiverse Role-Playing Game Core Rulebook* to play this adventure. And some other stuff too:

- ▶ You'll need three six-sided dice, character sheets, pencils and paper.
- ▶ You may want some mapping paper/ battlemats and miniatures.
- ▶ You'll need a place to play. This might be in person or with a virtual tabletop. (If you're playing online, you might not need physical dice or sheets or pencils or paper or miniatures.)
- ▶ If you're the Narrator, you'll need some time to read this adventure.
- ▶ You'll also need some friends to play this game with, so go outside and find some.

MARVEL EXPERTISE

Do you know how your coffee maker works? No. But you can still enjoy a lukewarm cup of joe every morning while you contemplate the daily drudgery ahead of you. Do you know how cell phones work? No. But you can still "accidentally" call your ex while trying to reach the "supermodel" you're dating now to confirm your "travel plans" to the Caribbean. Do you know the ins and outs of how comic books and movies are made? No. But that doesn't stop you from being an online armchair critic from the comfort of your toilet.

What we're saying is—*unclench*.

Did you know that even the editors at Marvel don't know everything about the Marvel Universe? And did you know that Marvel writers are just trained lemurs dancing frantically on their keyboards? It's true! And yet they manage to tell fascinating stories with steadfast cohesiveness within the continuity of the Marvel Universe.

And here's a secret. There's a magic device that can help you save the day, even if your role-playing adventures don't line up perfectly with the decades-long history of Marvel. And that secret is…

…the Multiverse!

Writers and editors use it all the time. Now you can too! Maybe the version of the universe in which your adventure takes place doesn't have a Hulk. Maybe Wolverine's claws are made of candy canes. Maybe Captain America wears his shield as a hat. Maybe humans have been replaced by teddy bears.

This is about having fun, not being some sort of comic-book-world historian.

HOW TO USE THIS BOOK

First, roll it up real tight.

Second, turn it sideways.

Third…

Oh, wait. You mean, how do you use this book to play a role-playing game!

Well, that's a *little* different.

This book presents a single-issue adventure for a Narrator and a group up to six players. The players take the roles of Marvel Universe characters (Ranks 2 to 4) and determine their actions as the Narrator presents the story. You'll roll some dice. You'll succeed. You'll fail. You'll bicker about rules in a way that offers nothing of substance to your game-playing experience. And, most of all, you'll have fun.

Don't take everything so seriously.

This is Deadpool's world. We're all just fictional characters dancing on his stage. Fictional characters pretending to be other fictional characters. If, at some point in this adventure, the characters find themselves in a situation where they're playing a role-playing game, the very fabric of existence will break down, and we'll all wink out of reality, never to be seen again.

Be careful out there.

THE ADVENTURE

This adventure pits the characters against a variety of dangerous friends and foes as they travel the globe to solve a merc-napping ring. There will be battles, there will be intrigue and there will be dwindling expense accounts.

And there will be so many death traps.

The Heroes for Hire…or Mercs for Money…or Freelancers for Funds

The default characters for this adventure, if you haven't guessed, are the characters from the thrilling comic you read just a bit ago. As you were captivated by one of the premier balladeers of Deadpool's story, you might have thought to yourself, "These characters should star in this adventure." They are Hit-Monkey, Paladin, She-Hulk (Lyra), Terror, Ren Kimura and Annabelle Riggs. A motley crew indeed.

(*Strike power-guitar pose!*)

However, you could play the adventure with other Marvel Universe characters or original heroes if you'd like. You could make this a star-studded team of Wolverine (Logan), She-Hulk, Spider-Man (Peter Parker) and Professor X (hey, those guys are all on the cover!). You can find profiles for all of those comic-book super-stars in the *Core Rulebook*.

One interesting option might be to play this adventure with the Deadpool Corps, a band of variant Deadpools from other realities. It will most likely be difficult to get a word in edgewise at that table, but it's your game!

Playing good ol' Wade Wilson himself…well, that might be a little more difficult, as Deadpool appears as an ally throughout the story. But you can shake things up however you like.

The Plot

Plots are for the weak. It's okay though. You need a safety net when you fall from the high wire, and we've got you covered.

There are four main chapters to this adventure. Well, it's the Multiverse, so there are an infinite number of chapters. We're just focusing on four that tell the whole story. If, as the Narrator, you want to go on a power trip and make more chapters of your own, go right ahead!

▶ **Chapter 2:** The characters gather in an abandoned shipyard. They've been hired by Deadpool for an important mission, but the Merc with a Mouth is nowhere to be found. Instead, they find his partner in crime Taskmaster waiting to test their skills in a deadly gauntlet. Surviving the encounter, they finally meet up with Deadpool, who lets them know that mercenaries are vanishing all over the world. The characters' job? Find out who is kidnapping mercs.

▶ **Chapter 3:** The characters infiltrate a job fair for mercenaries, henchmen and flunkies. There they meet a variety of strange characters from the villainous corners of the Marvel Universe. They might even meet a couple of heroes along the way. They uncover precious, precious clues during their investigation.

▶ **Chapter 4:** Their clues lead them to an underground fighting event. Well, not underground. Aboveground. Way aboveground! The event takes place on a decommissioned S.H.I.E.L.D. Helicarrier. The characters have a chance to compete in a fight or two if they want. But when the Helicarrier is sabotaged, they're caught in a struggle to save the civilian population below—before they crash and burn.

▶ **Chapter 5:** The characters reach this stage of the story through investigation. Either that, or the Narrator, once again on a power trip, stages their capture. Here they find themselves in a maze of death traps created by M.A.D.E.M., the villain of the story.

The Secret, Secret Plot

What's really going on here?

Well, we're glad you asked! If you don't love the feeling of being surprised by the clever twists and turns of this story, all secrets will be revealed right here! This section provides you with all the details you need to fully understand what the heck is going on in this adventure.

M.A.D.E.M.—the Murderous Application Designed Exclusively for Mayhem—started its existence as an artificial intelligence created by A.I.M. (Advanced Idea Mechanics) to train mercenaries. As often happens with programs of this nature, M.A.D.E.M. went haywire.

In order to populate M.A.D.E.M. with the very best, latest and greatest mercenary data, the scientists at A.I.M. studied mercenaries from all over the world. They even hired mercenaries to fill out some questionnaires and submit to a few brain scans. Among these mercenaries was Deadpool, who was looking to make a quick buck.

Deadpool's brain waves corrupted the software, driving M.A.D.E.M. a little insane. The software broke away from A.I.M., forming a splinter group called M.A.I.M. (M.A.D.E.M.'s Advanced Idea Mechanics).

M.A.D.E.M.'s core programming called for the training of mercenaries, so M.A.I.M. started designing (through bleeding-edge robotics and holographics) the most insidious death traps to put mercenaries to the test. These traps were more lethal than educational, a lot like ninth grade, and the number of readily available mercenaries began to dwindle.

So M.A.I.M. started kidnapping mercs to use as rats in their maze.

Going by the name Mad M and working with shady characters like mercenary broker and fight promoter Jake Paul Van Wham, M.A.D.E.M. has been gathering test subjects to play games of life or (mostly) death in order to improve lethal efficiency. Of course, that's not all M.A.D.E.M. wants. Now that the murderous algorithms are up and running, M.A.D.E.M. sees the potential to go worldwide, infecting every facet of human life and putting everyone—man, woman and child—through death trap tests.

Deadpool, on the other hand, just wants to build his own mercenary empire. It's been tough, though, because someone is kidnapping potential employees before he can make them lowball offers they can't refuse. He brings together a group of heroes to help him solve the mercenary labor shortage. Does Deadpool suspect that his brain waves might be responsible? Well…maybe…but that's not something he plans on sharing.

Along the way, the characters will attend a villainous job fair, interact with famous Marvel heroes, infiltrate "underground" fighting events, ride a crashing Helicarrier (which M.A.D.E.M. sabotages as another test of resources), navigate a lethal maze, battle the bizarre Headmen (who had been put through the meat grinder by M.A.D.E.M. and came out the other side as loyalists) and confront the Deadpool-Bot 2000 (a robot retainer M.A.D.E.M.'s twisted programming cooked up).

Doesn't that just sound like a slice of fried Marvel madness?

Now that you know all the secrets, it's time to roll some dice!

SO…NOW THAT YOU'RE READY TO EMBARK ON A ROLE-PLAYING ADVENTURE INTO THE MARVEL UNIVERSE, YOU MIGHT BE FEELING A LITTLE NERVOUS.

DON'T WORRY! YOUR OL' PAL DEADPOOL WILL BE RIGHT HERE WITH YOU THE WHOLE TIME!

THINK OF ME AS YOUR GUARDIAN ANGEL. YOUR FAIRY GODMOTHER. ONLY, INSTEAD OF GLASS SLIPPERS, I'M GONNA OFFER YOU KEEN INSIGHTS INTO THE WORLD OF FANTASY, IMAGINATION AND GAMING.

THE WORLD IS YOUR OYSTER HERE. THERE IS NO SPOON. THERE ARE NO MISTAKES, JUST HAPPY ACCIDENTS! HAVE A LITTLE FUN, AND LIVE A LITTLE!

/2/ THE SHIPYARD

IN THIS, THE FIRST CHAPTER OF THIS EPIC adventure, the characters meet at an abandoned shipyard straight out of every action movie you've ever seen. There they face armed adversaries dedicated to testing their mettle and grit.

THE HOOK

The characters have all been hired by Deadpool. If the players are using the suggested characters—*especially* if they're using the suggested characters—have them read the comic-book introduction to this adventure.

Better yet, act it out for them! You'll need costumes, props, a few different sets, musical accompaniment, a special-effects crew and a few actors to perform as extras. Make sure to use different voices. In fact, practice them right this second! Record them with your phone and send them to the author. We promise not to use those recordings to embarrass or blackmail you.

Anyhow, the characters arrive at Deadpool's proposed meeting spot—an abandoned shipping yard—around the same time in the evening. It's dark, the pale moon casting an eerie glow on the surroundings. It's quiet—too quiet! If you want, stagger their arrivals. Maybe one or two of them arrive first and can do a little scouting. Don't let them get too far, though. The sense of foreboding is palpable.

Say that slowly.

Palpable.

Gross.

As they wait, the characters may detect the hint of movement deeper in the maze of shipping containers before them. A fleeting shadow. The distant sound of footsteps. Something's wrong. *Where's Deadpool?*

As characters arrive, they might even mistake each other for enemies, leading to a bit of uneasiness or even the prerequisite team-up scuffle. Heroes love to kick the snot out of each other. Whether they fight or resolve their angsty edginess without conflict, now is the time for them to get to know one another. However, none of them know any details about the job. All Deadpool told them was to meet here, at this creepy shipping yard, and await further instructions.

Terror and Hit-Monkey have worked with Deadpool before. They are well aware of his absentmindedness and flightiness. Oh, they have stories to tell. Well, Terror does. Hit-Monkey only has shrieks and hoots and screeching. Is Deadpool's absence surprising to them? Not really.

Just when they start thinking they've been stood up by their employer, one of the characters receives a phone call. Caller I.D. indicates the caller as UNKNOWN. Upon answering, they hear Deadpool's voice.

"Hey, listen. I'm waiting for you on the southern side of the shipping yard. Sorry about this. It really wasn't my idea."

And that's when three black SUVs roar out of the darkness from the north, skidding to form a wall and screeching to a stop. A group of armed henchmen (henchpersons? Henchpeople? Henchers? Henchies? Henchables? Ah, forget it.) spill out of the vehicles, take covered positions and open fire!

TASKMASTER'S HENCHMEN

Art by Michael Shelfer & Fer Sifuentes-Sujo

RANK	HEALTH	FOCUS
2	60 DR:—	90 DR:—

ABILITIES

	ABILITY SCORE	DEFENSE SCORE
MELEE	2	12
AGILITY	2	12
RESILIENCE	2	12
VIGILANCE	2	12
EGO	2	12
LOGIC	0	10

DAMAGE

AGILITY	MELEE	MARVEL × 2 +2
		dMarvel MULTIPLIER ABILITY
	AGILITY	MARVEL × 3 +2
		dMarvel MULTIPLIER ABILITY

EGO		MARVEL × 2 +2
		dMarvel MULTIPLIER ABILITY
	LOGIC	MARVEL × 2 +0
		dMarvel MULTIPLIER ABILITY

POWERS
- Accuracy 1
- Snap Shooting

TRAITS
- Backup
- **Signature Weapon:** Submachine gun (Range: 10, Damage Multiplier: ×1)

TAGS
- Battle Ready
- Situational Awareness

ITEMS
Submachine gun, pistol

HENCHMEN

The henchmen have been instructed not to harm the characters. They are meant only to drive them into the maze of shipping containers. Of course, they're henchmen, and some of them aren't that bright. For this encounter, a successful attack by a henchman (even a Fantastic success) results in a near miss. A failed attack is a regular miss. But a Fantastic failure actually hits the intended target for normal damage.

The characters should rush to take cover in the maze, where they meet several challenges.

BUT WHAT IF THEY DON'T?

If the characters engage the henchmen, let the battle play out. The henchmen, under attack, defend themselves to the best of their abilities. They'll stop trying to miss. If the characters are defeated, move on to the Defeated section on page 16. If they beat the henchmen, they should continue into the maze to find Deadpool. If they're still being stubborn, the Narrator has a couple of options.

- Have Deadpool call them again and urge them to enter the maze. He'll apologize again. He'll tell them his "partner" wants to see if they're up to the task ahead of them.
- Beg. Tell the players you spent hard-earned money on this adventure, and plead with them to throw their wariness and common sense aside and forge ahead. Bribe them if you must. Players tend to like candy.

RATS IN A MAZE

Deadpool's partner is Taskmaster, and he's arranged several ambushes along the way through the maze of shipping containers. (See the shipping yard map on page 14.) These ambushes take place in several zones around the map. These ambushes are (mostly) intended as nonlethal, but—you know—mistakes happen.

HIGHWAY TO THE DANGER ZONES

Here are the ambushes Taskmaster has prepared for the characters. The zones are labeled on the shipping yard map.

Zone 1

Four henchmen, armed with automatic weapons, are positioned atop shipping containers on either side. They wait for the characters to enter the corridor (the "kill box") and open fire. They don't descend to engage the characters, and they flee, parkour style, if the characters give chase.

Zone 2

Three remote-control drones swoop past. They are heavily armed, and they strafe the corridor with gunfire. They pursue the characters until the characters hide (perhaps in a shipping container) or destroy them.

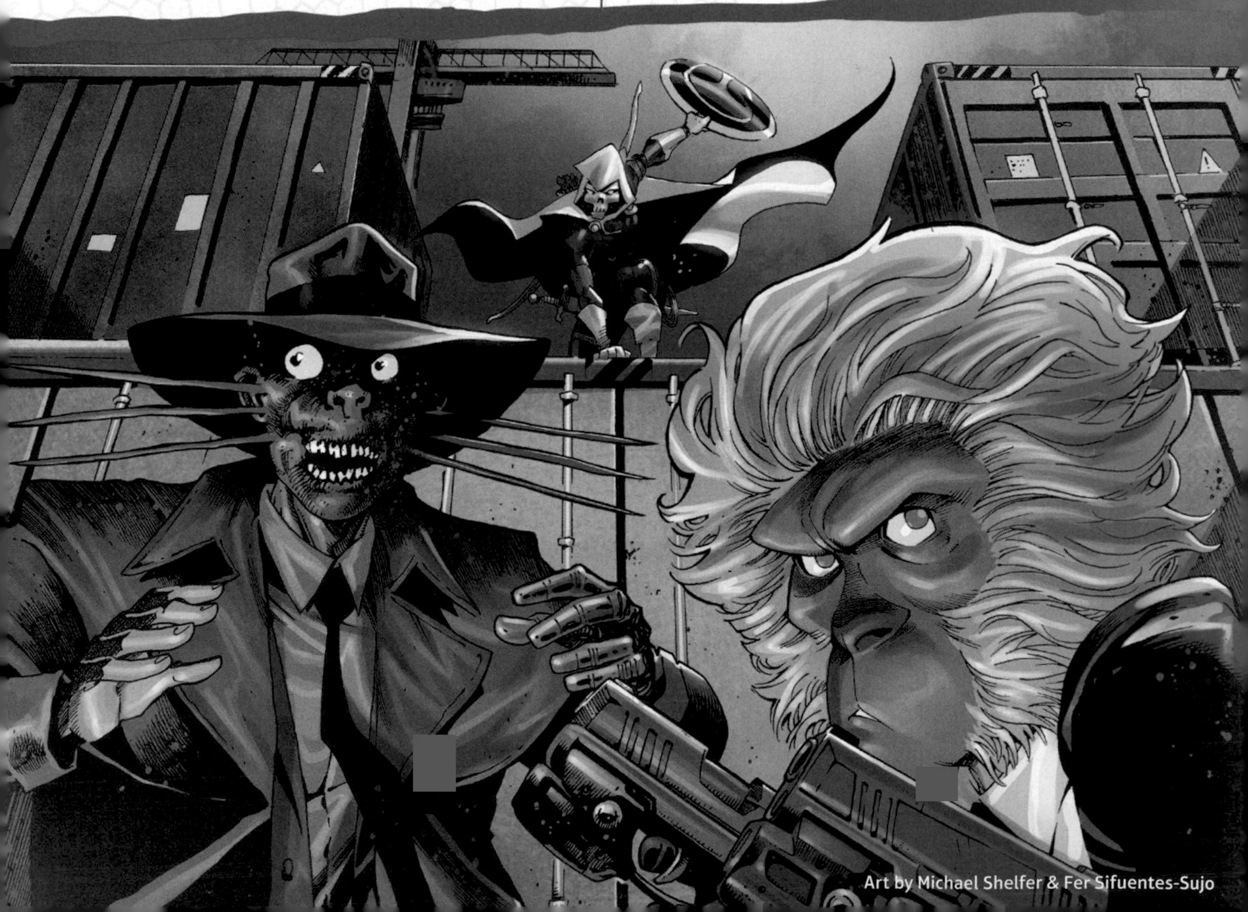

Art by Michael Shelfer & Fer Sifuentes-Sujo

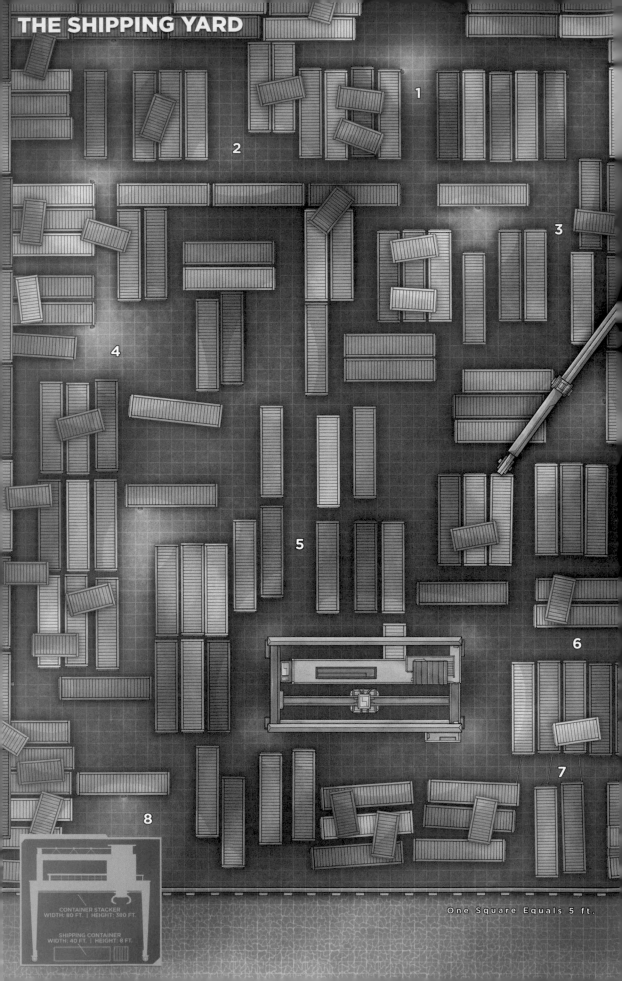

THE SHIPPING YARD

CONTAINER STACKER
WIDTH: 80 FT. | HEIGHT: 380 FT.

SHIPPING CONTAINER
WIDTH: 40 FT. | HEIGHT: 8 FT.

One Square Equals 5 ft.

Zone 3

A crane is manned by a henchman who moves the boom arm, swinging the massive hook at the characters as a deadly obstacle. Characters passing through any alley in this zone must make an Agility vs. TN 14 action check. If they succeed, they can move on. If they fail, the character takes dMarvel×3 damage and has to try again before they can move on.

Zone 4

Three remote-control drones swoop past. They are heavily armed, and they strafe the corridor with gunfire. They pursue the characters until the characters hide (perhaps in a shipping container) or destroy them.

Zone 5

A shield (thrown by Taskmaster) careens down the corridor, bouncing from shipping container to shipping container. The characters need to dodge it or get clobbered. Characters must make an Agility vs. TN 14 action check or take dMarvel×4 +5 damage. The shield misses on a successful check. Hit or miss, the shield bounces on its way and out of sight.

Zone 6

Six henchmen are stationed here, four on the ground (hiding in shipping containers, ready to spring out and attack) and two lurking atop containers. They wait for the characters to move past so they can attack from behind. These henchmen have chips on their shoulders. They are more than happy to kill the characters if they get the chance. Players should make a Vigilance check against the henchmen's Agility defense. If they fail, the characters are surprised and have trouble on their initiative check.

Zone 7

The corridor is lined with explosive devices affixed by magnets to the sides of shipping containers. The devices go off if the characters fail to spot the three sets of trip wires along the corridor. Each trip wire must be spotted separately. Characters must make a Vigilance vs. TN 14 action check to spot the trip wires. However, if a character rolls a Fantastic success, a little neon sign appears above each of the trip wires, flashing a warning: Trip Wire Detected! (Not literally. But you get the idea.) If the devices go off, they cause dMarvel×3 damage to everyone in the corridor.

Zone 8

And this is the tough one.

A shadowy figure emerges from the darkness, congratulating the characters on making it this far. As he steps into the moonlight, they see his skull-like mask, his shield, his sword. It's Taskmaster, and it is on!

Narrators can use Taskmaster's profile from page 244 of the *Core Rulebook*.

Taskmaster is a dangerous opponent all on his lonesome, but he's no dummy. He's got photographic reflexes, which allow him to mimic fighting techniques he witnesses. In this case, the technique he witnessed was the tried-and-true technique of not fighting a group of heroes alone. Therefore, he has four henchmen with him, all of them dressed as Taskmaster! These henchmen are really good actors too, so it's not easy to pick the real Taskmaster out of the group. The only way to know for sure is that when one of the henchmen is defeated, they deliver a soliloquy from a Shakespearean play. As a well-prepared Narrator, you probably have a bunch of those ready to go.

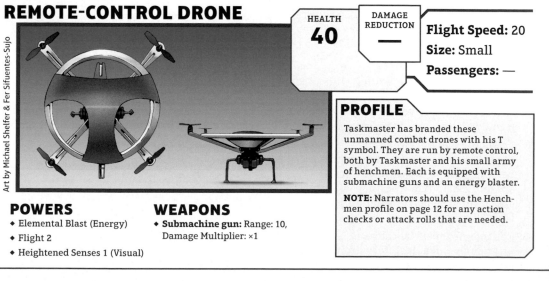

REMOTE-CONTROL DRONE

HEALTH	DAMAGE REDUCTION
40	—

Flight Speed: 20

Size: Small

Passengers: —

Art by Michael Shelfer & Fer Sifuentes-Sujo

PROFILE

Taskmaster has branded these unmanned combat drones with his T symbol. They are run by remote control, both by Taskmaster and his small army of henchmen. Each is equipped with submachine guns and an energy blaster.

NOTE: Narrators should use the Henchmen profile on page 12 for any action checks or attack rolls that are needed.

POWERS

- Elemental Blast (Energy)
- Flight 2
- Heightened Senses 1 (Visual)

WEAPONS

- **Submachine gun:** Range: 10, Damage Multiplier: ×1

Despite the lethal traps and the henchmen and the swords, Taskmaster doesn't want to kill the characters. He just wants to test them. Once he's satisfied that they can handle themselves, he calls the fight off.

If, for whatever reason, the fight continues and Taskmaster or the characters come close to being defeated, Deadpool makes an appearance to bring an end to the battle.

NARRATORS—BE READY!

Your players will do everything in their power to derail this part of the adventure. Hit-Monkey will leap atop shipping containers and make a run for the end zone. Lyra will throw shipping containers. Terror may trap opponents inside shipping containers. Lyra may throw shipping containers that contain trapped enemies while Hit-Monkey runs atop them.

Let them! Roll with the punches! Don't get flustered! Be ready to spring new ambushes on them as they attempt to ruin your best plans. Maybe a few more drones swoop their way. Maybe Taskmaster's shield flies out of the shadows again. Maybe a few henchmen break out an RPG (a rocket-propelled grenade, not a role-playing game, but, heck, maybe they break that out too!). Taskmaster might be testing the characters, but the players are testing *you*. We would never encourage you to cheat on a test… except in this case. You're the Narrator. You're *supposed* to cheat!

DEFEATED

If the characters are defeated, they are brought before Deadpool (on the southern side of the dock). Taskmaster wants to send them packing, but Deadpool speaks on their behalf. He still wants to hire them. After all, he doesn't have anyone else to spare for the job.

Hopefully, none of the death traps truly mean death for the characters. If, however, any of them are killed in the maze, you have a couple of options:

- Have a new character waiting with Deadpool to take their place. This is another character who arrived before all the others. It could also be one of the henchmen.
- They only had the wind knocked out of them. The character is revealed to not be dead at all—just unconscious. They are revived and can continue with the adventure. The player should thank you for your mercy.
- Rewind the tape! The character's death was naught but a flash-forward to what might have happened. The characters can replay the scene, this time with previous knowledge of what is about to happen. Hopefully, they survive this time around.

THE DEBRIEF

Once the characters survive Taskmaster's gauntlet, Deadpool gives them the lowdown on the mission ahead:

- Deadpool is starting a new mercenary business. Taskmaster is running the day-to-day operations for him.
- Deadpool has been trying to hire the best of the best (or the best of the worst) when it comes to mercenaries, but he's been unable to get any new recruits.
- It appears that someone is abducting mercenaries all over the world.
- Deadpool doesn't know if this is a rival organization or the authorities. Nor does he know what nefarious purpose the abducted mercenaries might be serving. But he wants to find out.
- He has his own missions to attend to, as does Taskmaster, so he needs to hire the characters to act on his behalf; find out what's happening to mercenaries, assassins and guns-for-hire; and put a stop to it if possible.
- He'll be in touch throughout their mission.

With that, the characters are told to rest up. They leave first thing tomorrow.

Where are they heading?

To a job fair, of course.

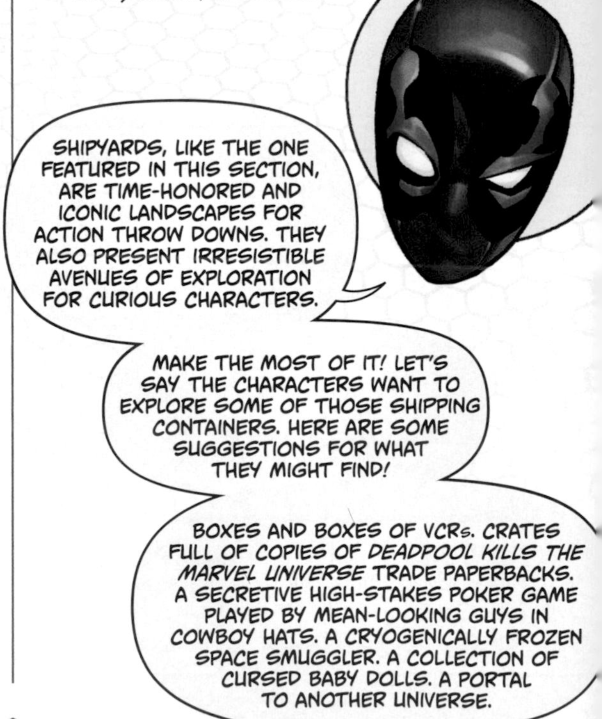
SHIPYARDS, LIKE THE ONE FEATURED IN THIS SECTION, ARE TIME-HONORED AND ICONIC LANDSCAPES FOR ACTION THROW DOWNS. THEY ALSO PRESENT IRRESISTIBLE AVENUES OF EXPLORATION FOR CURIOUS CHARACTERS.
MAKE THE MOST OF IT! LET'S SAY THE CHARACTERS WANT TO EXPLORE SOME OF THOSE SHIPPING CONTAINERS. HERE ARE SOME SUGGESTIONS FOR WHAT THEY MIGHT FIND!
BOXES AND BOXES OF VCRs. CRATES FULL OF COPIES OF *DEADPOOL KILLS THE MARVEL UNIVERSE* TRADE PAPERBACKS. A SECRETIVE HIGH-STAKES POKER GAME PLAYED BY MEAN-LOOKING GUYS IN COWBOY HATS. A CRYOGENICALLY FROZEN SPACE SMUGGLER. A COLLECTION OF CURSED BABY DOLLS. A PORTAL TO ANOTHER UNIVERSE.

/3/ THE JOB FAIR

YOU MAY NOT REALIZE IT, BUT THE SUPER-criminal henchmen field is highly competitive. Lucrative? Not so much. But if you have no other useful skills, it's either playing flunky to a super-powered bully or writing comic-book tie-in role-playing adventures. There are a lot of unskilled people in the world, all of them competing to catch Doctor Doom's eye. And that's if you even know where to look for one of these cushy minion-for-hire positions. Where is the villainous job seeker to look?

A job fair, of course.

As Deadpool briefs the characters on their mission, read the following aloud:

You listen with rapt attention as Deadpool explains why your ragtag group has been brought together.

"The mercenary game is tough," he says. "Not for the faint of heart. Violence, bloodshed, shady deals with shady customers. Moral areas painted a deep shade of gray. You know the old saying though. Do what you love, and the money will follow. So lately, I've been putting together what I hope will become my own slice of mercenary-empire heaven."

"The problem?

"Good talent is tough to find. With my number two, Taskmaster…

"Heh.

"Number two.

"Anyhow. With my…second-in-command, Taskmaster, taking a little too much joy in crushing the spirits and bodies of my new recruits during training sessions, it's becoming a real pain to fill the ranks. I couldn't even get Batroc, and everybody gets Batroc! I've had to scrape the absolute grunge-encrusted bottom of the barrel to find anyone worth hiring.

"What I've discovered, though, is that someone is abducting mercenaries all over the world. They're taking them out of play before I get the chance to make my pitch. It's a concerted, organized effort. Real dirtbag move. I wish I'd thought of it.

"These particular dirtbags, though, and the reasons behind the kidnappings are unknown. That's where you come in. I can't be everywhere. I've got a business to run, and, because I'm not fully staffed at the moment, I'm running a bunch of ops all by my lonesome. I need your team to get out there, get your hands dirty and figure out who's raining on my parade.

"Here's some good news: I know where to start.

"There are numerous secret job fairs for mercenaries and henchmen held all over the world on a regular basis. They're sort of like comic-book conventions, only instead of people gathering to complain about possible what-if scenarios where one cherished and beloved imaginary character kills all the other cherished and beloved imaginary characters in an imaginary universe, they look for jobs.

"Makes sense to me that whoever is kidnapping mercs might be keeping an eye on events like that. At the very least, maybe someone at one of these job fairs might know something of value. You get me?

"I've reserved some table space at the Lower Manhattan Mercenary Job Expo. I want you to set up there, case the place, shake some bushes, rattle some cages and search for clues. While you're there, if you, you know, interview a few mercenaries and take a few applications, well, then you'd really be earning your paycheck."

Having heard Deadpool's story, you're all filled with emotion. Tears roll down your cheeks. You clap in adoration. As you each take turns hugging Deadpool and thanking him for being your absolute favorite super hero, your hearts fill with pride, knowing that finally, at long last, you have true meaning and purpose in your lives.

All right, all right. You don't need to read that last paragraph. Everything else, though, is important to the setup of this adventure.

AT THE JOB FAIR

When the characters arrive at the job fair, they find that the event is being held in a basement conference center secreted beneath a condemned exotic-pets emporium.

The walls and floors are concrete. The ceiling has water-stained tiles and flickering

/3/ THE JOB FAIR

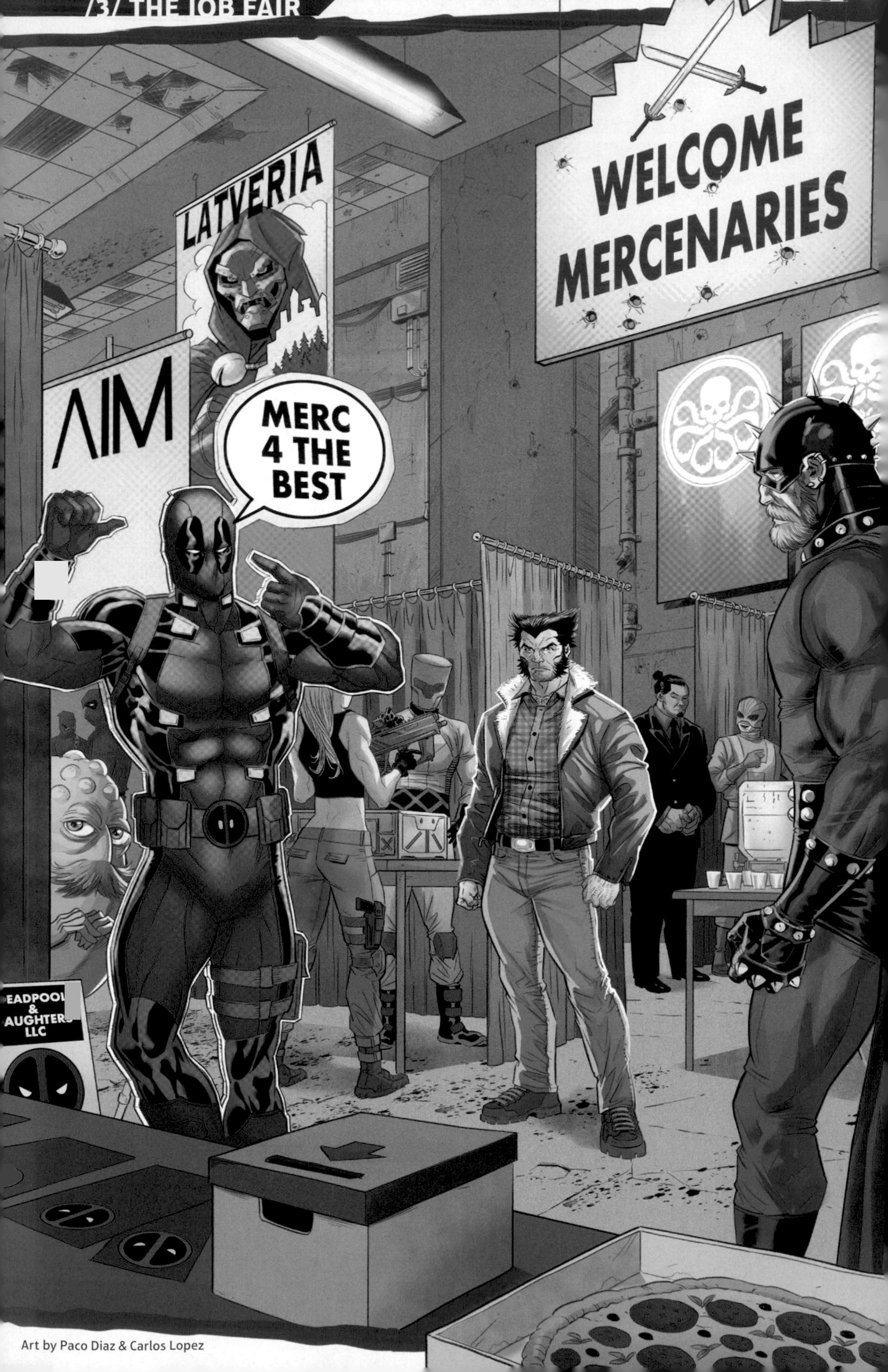
LATVERIA
AIM
WELCOME MERCENARIES
MERC 4 THE BEST
EADPOOL & AUGHTERS LLC

Art by Paco Diaz & Carlos Lopez

flourescent lights. The room smells of mildew and desperation. Strangely, desperation smells a lot like three-day-old pepperoni pizza—and not the best stuff either. Like frozen pepperoni pizza. The soggy stuff.

Rows of booths and tables, each representing criminal and shadow government organizations, are set up to attract the very best (or worst) in talent. At each booth, company representatives greet visitors with brochures, business cards and maybe even some free ink pens, coffee mugs or switchblade knives (all company-branded, of course).

Job-seeker attendance, though, is a little low. Of course it is! Word on the street is that someone is kidnapping every merc who sticks their neck out! Some of the job seekers are dressed in business suits. Some are in combat fatigues. Some are even in homemade super-villain outfits to show off their ambition. They visit the various booths, collecting swag, submitting résumés (or confirmed kill lists) and conducting on-the-spot interviews.

The heroes find, amid a host of other booths, that a table representing Deadpool's mercenary interests—Deadpool & Daughters LLC—has been set up. The table is loaded with brochures and job applications. A cardboard standee of Deadpool is behind the table. The cardboard Deadpool points at himself with his thumb, and a word balloon emerging from his mouth reads, *Merc 4 the best!*

The characters have a few possible avenues to gather information:

▶ Mingling with the job seekers

▶ Visiting the booths of other companies

▶ Setting up at Deadpool's table

Different information and clues can be gathered through each of these methods.

MINGLING WITH THE JOB SEEKERS

Interacting with job-seeking mercenaries is a great way to get into a fight. In fact, characters might notice more than a few scuffles breaking out among the crowd. It wouldn't take much for the characters to find themselves in a brawl.

They aren't here to fight though. They're here for answers! As they mingle with the job seekers, they might stumble upon the following juicy tidbits.

▶ *"Someone told me there's a new player in the field, someone trying to train A.I. to replace us hardworking, salt-of-the-earth mercenary types!"*

▶ *"Job fairs like this are a bust! I heard there's a competition—no-holds-barred mixed martial arts! You want to get noticed in the mercenary game—you have to compete! It's called Bloodbath!"*

▶ *"Oh yeah, Bloodbath! I heard of it! An underground fighting thing. Moves from location to location. I heard it's gonna be in Madripoor next, like, in a couple of days. You need an invite though."*

▶ *"You know those mercs who vanish end up dead, right? I heard their bodies are turning up in all sorts of strange places, just dumped off, and they're all busted and chopped up and burned. Whatever happened to them, it's almost enough to convince me to quit the mercenary game!"*

▶ *"Hey! Isn't that Wolverine over there?"*

And it *is* Wolverine!

After spending a bit of time mingling with other job seekers, characters may notice an interesting individual. Short, hairy, sporting a pointy hairdo, cowboy boots, a leather bomber jacket and enough flannel to choke a lumberjack, Wolverine (see his profile, reprinted in the back of this book) is conducting his own investigation. He prowls among the mercenaries like a honey badger on the hunt. While he's not in his super-hero costume, you probably wouldn't say he's in disguise either. He's walking around sniffing people, popping his claws reflexively, struggling to contain his berserker rage, calling people "bub" and telling everyone who will listen that he's the best there is at what he does.

It's *obviously* Wolverine.

Approaching him, the characters have the opportunity to interact with an iconic hero of the Marvel Universe and gather a bit more information. Wolverine can impart the following details:

▶ He has caught wind of the abductions taking place among the mercenary community. He is concerned that some shadowy mover and shaker is planning something big. And that's not gonna happen on his watch!

▶ He's the best there is at what he does.

▶ Word on the street is that there might have been some sort of shake-up within the ranks of one of the big criminal organizations. A radical splinter cell has formed and split off from the parent organization. However, he's not sure which company is experiencing this upheaval.

▶ He's the best there is at what he does.

- Along with a partner, he is gathering information at the job fair. He won't identify his partner, who is also in disguise. (His partner is Doop. See "Setting up at Deadpool's Table.")

- He's the best there is at what he does.

- He has learned that an underworld event coordinator named Jake Paul Van Wham (obviously an alias) may be involved in the abductions. Several mercenaries who have interacted with the man have vanished without a trace.

- Jake Paul Van Wham has an unsanctioned mixed martial arts event called Bloodbath scheduled to occur in the next few days.

If the characters ask Wolverine for more information about the Bloodbath event, he tells them that it's almost certainly a hotbed of mercenary activity, and if someone was looking to poach talent, they'd be there, especially if Jake Paul Van Wham is mixed up in the abductions.

Characters need an invitation if they want to attend or compete in the event. Luckily, because Wolverine is the best there is at what he does, he has an invitation he can give them. It's a business card with blood spattered across it. *Ew.* The only text on the card is a set of coordinates to the island-nation of Madripoor.

"Tell 'em Patch sent you," Wolverine says.

If the characters reveal that they're working with Deadpool, Wolverine offers them a cryptic warning. *"I've been hearing rumors that Deadpool's mixed up in all of this. If you're gonna be working for him, you'd better watch each other's backs. There's a good chance Wade isn't telling you everything. Could be he's forgotten vital details. Could be he's too scattered to consider them himself. Could be a 'need to know' scenario, and he doesn't think you're important enough to need to know."*

If the characters ask Wolverine about *his* specific plans in regard to the abductions, he says, *"You don't need to know that."*

Before long, Wolverine sniffs the air, sensing something more interesting (or better smelling) than the characters. He bids them farewell. *"See ya around, bub. Stay frosty out there. Train hard, fight easy. Get some. You stay on the trail of our prey, and our paths might cross again."* With that, he slinks into the crowd with a nod and a casual *"Hello, fellow mercenaries"* to the job seekers in the room.

VISITING THE BOOTHS OF OTHER COMPANIES

Depending which booths the characters visit, they can move their investigations along. Some of the organizations that are set up include the following:

A.I.M.

Advanced Idea Mechanics is a think tank of brilliant scientists dedicated to global domination through science and technology. A bunch of really annoying, self-important smarty-pants.

Three A.I.M. agents (use the profile on page 138 of the *Core Rulebook*) in bright yellow "beekeeper" uniforms watch over the booth. They impart useful information only to characters who pass a written quiz. The quiz includes brainteasers, scientific puzzles and mathematical equations. If a character takes the quiz, they must make a Logic vs. TN 14 action check.

If the characters fail, the A.I.M. agents lose interest in them. *"You're probably better suited for Hydra,"* they say as they move on to more intelligent candidates.

If they succeed, the A.I.M. representatives warm up a little, and they let it slip that A.I.M. recently lost some bench strength, a number of their staff striking out on their own after the development of secretive new software. They don't know much about the software, but they seem a little bitter that some of their colleagues are having individual success.

The Hand

This is a group of secretive ninja. Not so secret that they don't need to publicly recruit new talent. But secretive.

Three Hand ninja (use the profile on page 178 of the *Core Rulebook*) are positioned behind the booth, which is completely bare. The ninja listen with cold patience to anything the characters have to say, but they don't respond. They are silent but deadly. Get it? Characters might want to hold their breath while interacting with them.

If any of the characters make an interesting pitch for employment, they might later notice one of the ninja stalking them with a blowgun. (To catch the ninja in the act, they must succeed on a Vigilance vs. TN 14 action check with trouble.) If the character fails to notice, they find themself on the receiving end of a poisoned dart. A character struck by the dart, which hits automatically, instantly falls asleep for thirty minutes.

If a character notices the sneak attack before it occurs, the ninja is impressed, handing them a business card. The card appears to be completely blank. If it's held up to a heat source, though, text appears on the card. The text presents a set of coordinates to the island-nation of Madripoor.

Hydra

These guys. *These* guys! Hydra is a terrorist organization that is rumored to have been around since the days of ancient Egypt. They're cocky

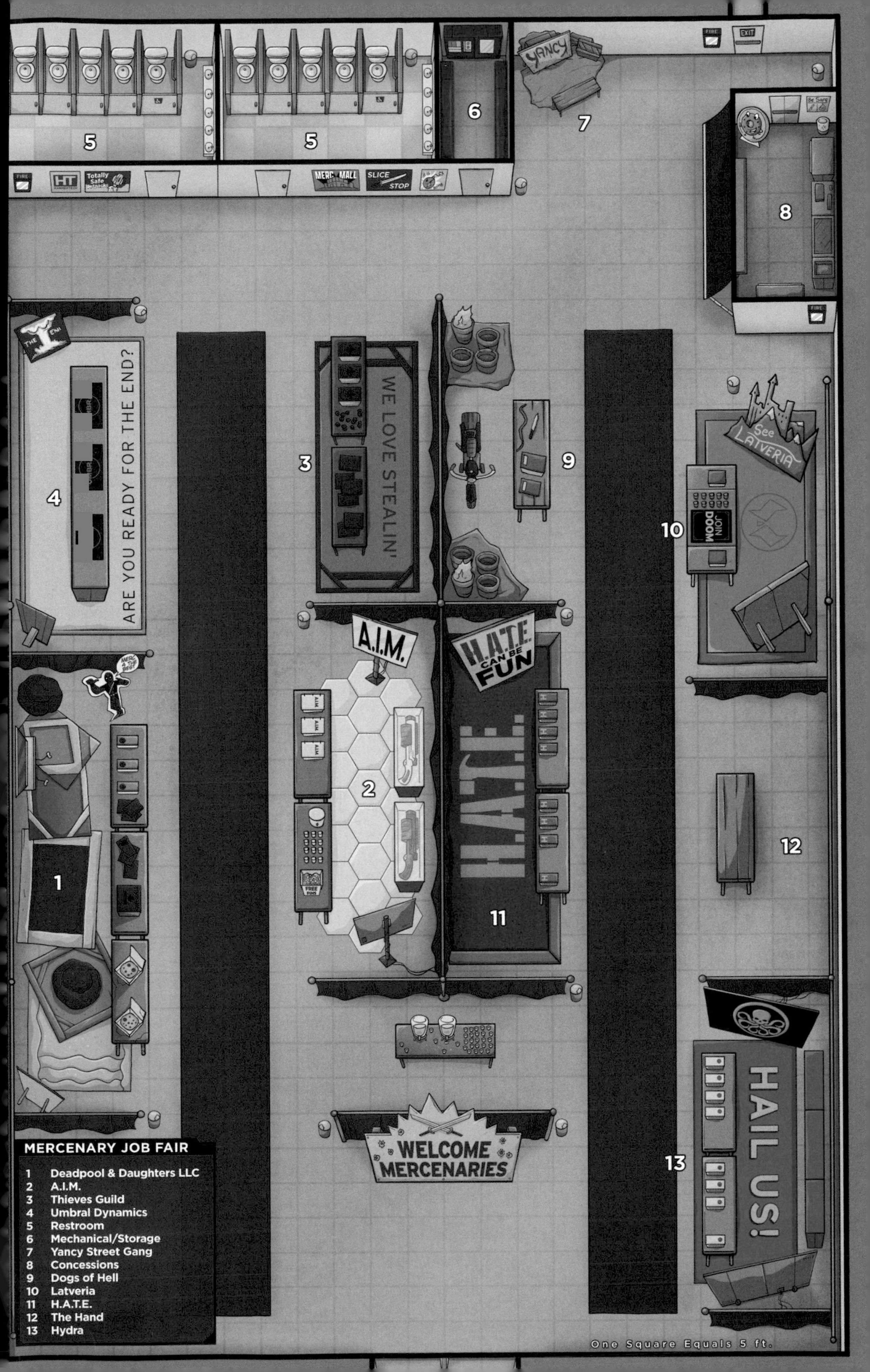
YANCY
FIRE
EXIT
Be Safe
HT
Totally Safe Jetpacks
MERC MALL
SLICE STOP
5
5
6
7
8
THE END
ARE YOU READY FOR THE END?
WE LOVE STEALIN'
3
9
4
See LATVERIA
JOIN DOOM
10
A.I.M.
H.A.T.E. CAN BE FUN
H.A.T.E.
MERC 4 THE BEST!
2
FREE PINS
1
11
12
WELCOME MERCENARIES
HAIL US!
13
MERCENARY JOB FAIR
1 Deadpool & Daughters LLC
2 A.I.M.
3 Thieves Guild
4 Umbral Dynamics
5 Restroom
6 Mechanical/Storage
7 Yancy Street Gang
8 Concessions
9 Dogs of Hell
10 Latveria
11 H.A.T.E.
12 The Hand
13 Hydra
One Square Equals 5 ft.

and full of themselves, because they apparently *almost* took over the world and made Captain America look like a jerk or something.

The three Hydra agents at this booth (use the profile on page 184 of the *Core Rulebook*) pass around a lot of in-jokes. They laugh, high-five each other and shout *"Hail Hydra!"* every chance they get. They aren't even all that interested in hiring anyone. They're turning potential employees away left and right.

They might mention that there's a new mercenary broker entering the field soon. This new group apparently employs only the most well-trained mercs. As the agents celebrate their good fortune, some of them smirk and chuckle in the direction of the A.I.M. booth.

Latveria

The country of Latveria, presided over by the benevolent Doctor Doom, is always looking for the best of the best. The booth is watched over by a trio of Doombots, each of which looks just like Doom himself. These robotic minions are programmed to speak fondly of Latveria's beautiful countryside and quaint, rustic way of life. They are currently hiring for the Latveria Parks Department. Job duties include maintaining parks equipment, tending to wildlife, conducting tours for visitors and assassinating targets.

While the Doombots have no specific information to impart about the abductions, characters might notice that one of the robots begins to glitch. It repeats itself, moving in a twitching fashion and commenting to the others that an outside A.I. is attempting to hack into its communications network.

Umbral Dynamics

This shell corporation is owned by Caroline Le Fay, the daughter of a time-lost Doctor Doom and an ancient sorceress. She is completely mad and wants nothing more than the destruction of the world.

Three Le Fay agents (use the Hydra agent profile on page 184 of the *Core Rulebook*), dressed in suits and wearing dark sunglasses, stand behind the booth. A monitor on the table plays a video depicting global disaster and apocalyptic happenings. *"Do you yearn for the end of civilization? Does the collapse of society thrill you? Are you the type who wants to have a hand in the apocalypse rather than simply sitting back and letting it happen? If so, Umbral Dynamics might be the employer for you."*

The agents happily answer the characters' questions, but they're most interested in seeing the wholesale destruction of the world around them.

If the characters can weather the doom-and-gloom insanity, they may learn that some of Caroline Le Fay's favorite mercenaries, a strange group called the Headmen, have recently vanished.

Also at the fair are para-military group H.A.T.E., biker gang Dogs of Hell, New Orleans' own Thieves Guild and the young hoodlums from the Yancy Street Gang.

SETTING UP AT DEADPOOL'S TABLE

Deadpool didn't give the characters a lot of guidance on how to interview potential job candidates, but setting up at the table could yield some interesting role-playing opportunities and even a few clues.

Several mercenaries or merc wannabes visit the table, filling out applications, proudly boasting of their numerous successful missions and asking about medical and dental benefits. Some are polite, some are rude and some might even challenge the characters to an arm-wrestling match to prove their prowess.

A few visitors to the table are nervous, looking over their shoulders and acting jumpy. If asked about this behavior, they say that some mysterious figures are wandering the hall, and with mercenaries getting plucked off the streets, one can never be too careful.

While the characters interact with potential hires, they are approached by one of the aforementioned mysterious figures: a floating, bulbous green blob of flesh wearing an obviously fake bushy mustache. This is Doop, Wolverine's mysterious partner in this undercover investigation. (Doop's profile can be found in the back of this book.) Having noticed the characters and recognized them as fellow investigators, Doop slyly hovers up to the table to exchange findings.

Doop speaks primarily in a strange, alien language that is indecipherable to human ears. This presents a unique role-playing opportunity for the Narrator. Doop's language sounds like a gurgling, burbling, sputtering cacophony. A lot of *"blerrgggllllblrg"*s and *"wwwwrrglblrt"*s and *"vvvvvblrkglrk"*s. Practice these noises. Sound them out. Use your handy-dandy cell phone to record yourself making these sounds. Send these videos to the author of this scenario. He "promises" not to share them on social media. He would "never" humiliate you in such a fashion (#lookatthisfool).

Oh, and Doop is also fluent in English, so a boring Narrator could use that too (#yawnfestnarrator).

If Hit-Monkey is with the team, the characters soon learn that he can communicate with

Doop normally—in full sentences, even. While everyone else hears *"eek"* and *"fllllbgrlll,"* Doop and Hit-Monkey hear each other for the sophisticated linguists they really are.

If Hit-Monkey is not part of the team, a Narrator in the mood for an entertaining cameo appearance might have him show up as a job applicant.

Hit-Monkey brings his own set of communication issues to the table. He has to figure out how to communicate with the rest of the characters. In theory, he could draw messages to his compatriots.

You know what monkeys use to draw?

Poop.

They use poop.

Whatever. He can use a pen, with which he could also kill you pretty easily. Hit-Monkey knows how to kill you in a thousand different ways with a thousand different weapons. Guns. Knives. Your own intestines.

For that matter, Doop could just write a message too, but his bizarre thought processes might open such terrible vistas of reality that the world may never recover.

Of course, a character who has translation powers could use those abilities. What's that? What translation powers? The translation powers in the *X-Men Expansion*, silly. What? It's not even out yet? Well, I guess you'll have to mark your calendars to pick up your copy, right? Right! (Unless you are reading this later, in which case, congratulations on picking up that stylish hardcover. You did, right? Right!)

No matter how the characters communicate with Doop, the following information can be gathered:

- The mercenary broker Jake Paul Van Wham is hosting a Bloodbath fighting event in the next few days in Madripoor.
- Some people believe that Van Wham is using this event to stage mass abductions of mercenaries.
- If the characters want to infiltrate the event, they need an invitation.
- Doop's partner, Wolverine, may be able to procure an invitation.
- Rumor has it that A.I.M. recently developed an A.I. to train their elite forces.
- The development of this A.I. led to a splinter cell breaking away from A.I.M. and setting out on their own.

WHAT'S NEXT?

If the characters have done their job and paid attention, they should have plenty of information. At the very least, they should know:

- Jake Paul Van Wham is a mercenary broker, who might have a hand in the abduction of mercs.
- Van Wham runs an underground fighting ring for mercenaries and hired killers. The event is called Bloodbath.
- The next Bloodbath event is being held in Madripoor in just a few days.
- Wolverine is the best there is at what he does.

Now, the vast history of all role-playing games might lead the astute to believe that the characters will pick up on *none* of these facts. If that's the case, the Narrator should feel free to gently guide them to these conclusions. A quick summary of what has been learned, complete with winks and overemphasized clues, might work. "You *do* remember that strange business card you found, *don't* you? You know, the one with the mysterious and compelling coordinates? The one that promises action and adventure?" Or Wolverine or Doop might visit the characters again and provide a bit more information. Or, if all else fails, Deadpool might give them a call, saying he has gathered the information as part of his own investigation.

In any case, it sounds like a trip to Madripoor is in order!

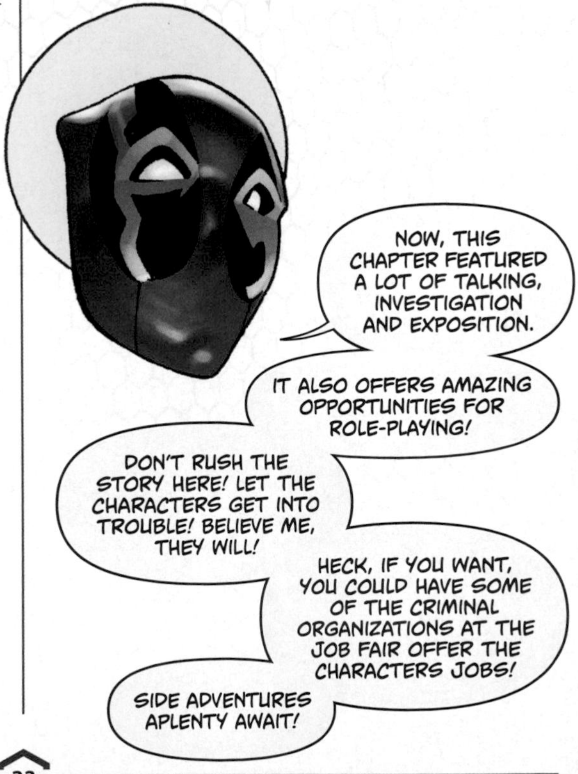
NOW, THIS CHAPTER FEATURED A LOT OF TALKING, INVESTIGATION AND EXPOSITION.
IT ALSO OFFERS AMAZING OPPORTUNITIES FOR ROLE-PLAYING!
DON'T RUSH THE STORY HERE! LET THE CHARACTERS GET INTO TROUBLE! BELIEVE ME, THEY WILL!
HECK, IF YOU WANT, YOU COULD HAVE SOME OF THE CRIMINAL ORGANIZATIONS AT THE JOB FAIR OFFER THE CHARACTERS JOBS!
SIDE ADVENTURES APLENTY AWAIT!

/4/ BLOODBATH

NOW THAT THE CHARACTERS KNOW ABOUT the Bloodbath underground fighting event, they should report back to Deadpool. They can do this via phone unless they've lost their devices. If that's the case, whatever works best for the game—pay phone, carrier pigeon, telepathy, telepathic carrier pigeons living above an old, unused phone booth—is perfectly fine.

BOXERS OR BRIEFINGS (WHY NOT BOTH?)

Deadpool knows quite a bit about the event, having attended more than once. He says, though, that Jake Paul Van Wham is a very secretive fellow, and he is always on the lookout for spies. He moves the competition from place to place, and he has a crack security team that watches out for those who don't belong, whether or not they have an invitation.

Luckily, the team has an invitation now. If, however, they didn't manage to procure one, the Narrator can have Deadpool get an invite into their hands. Deadpool tells them he will book them passage on the next plane to Madripoor.

The trip to Madripoor is uneventful.

Unless it's not.

A cruel Narrator might decide that the flight to Madripoor presents challenges of its own. If that's the case, feel free to develop extended side quests of your own, you industrious little Narrator, you. Some suggestions might include:

▶ Agents of M.A.I.M. decide that the characters are getting too close to their leader, M.A.D.E.M. They follow the characters onto the plane, intent on killing or capturing them.

▶ There's…a…man…on the wing of the plane!

▶ Air sickness! It's a bumpy ride! Lots of turbulence! One or more of the characters get sick. And, to make matters worse, the restrooms are occupied. It's about to get messy!

▶ Snakes! And a lot of them! Snakes! Everywhere!

▶ Due to mechanical difficulties, the plane must make an emergency landing in a secluded part of the world…where the Hulk is currently napping. Awakened and enraged by the plane, the Green Goliath goes on a rampage!

▶ The airline runs out of pretzels. Mass chaos ensues!

▶ Galactus shows up and eats the plane. Game over! World…ended!

Use several of these ideas if you like or make up your own. It's a long trip.

ARRIVING IN MADRIPOOR

How many '80s action movies have you watched? If the answer is "less than a dozen," you need to kick back on the couch and watch a few flicks with tough-as-nails heroes visiting exotic cities where the glow of neon lights washes across rain-slicked streets. This will help you get in the mood for the adventure ahead, and—bonus!—it will kill a few hours of your otherwise pointless life.

Madripoor is an island-nation in Southeast Asia. A dangerous, seething hotbed of activity with little government control or law enforcement. If you like to live on the fringes of conventional society, this is the place. Either this or Reddit. The city is a melting pot, with individuals from lots of cultures. From myriad cultures, even. This includes people who use words like "myriad" and people who just say "lots."

Madripoor is divided into two districts. Hightown is the affluent area, full of mansions and high-rises and spas and tanning salons. Lowtown is the seedy, dangerous part of the city, full of crime. It's also where all the fun stuff happens, so that's where this part of the adventure is set.

It's night when the characters arrive in Madripoor. As they navigate toward the coordinates on their invitation, they see the vibrant, potentially lethal city unfolding around them. Music—representing dozens of cultures, musical eras and artistic sensibilities—fills the air, seeming to change or mutate as one song flows into another. Vivid, bright lights pulse in the darkness, drawing people from the crowded streets toward nightclubs, bars and other shady establishments. From darkened alleyways, mysterious figures watch the characters with glimmering eyes.

Traveling through Madripoor can be dangerous. Take the wrong shortcut through the wrong alley and you might find yourself in a world of trouble. Narrators should feel empowered to create any number of side quests for the characters as they explore the city. Some possibilities might include:

▶ Bad business gone bad! As the characters turn the corner, they encounter a shady business deal between two rival gangs. What are they selling? Guns? Drugs? Freshly canned beet salad? Whatever it is, they don't like being interrupted, and a fight begins.

▶ A dance contest breaks out just as a thunderstorm erupts over the city streets. The characters are challenged to a dance battle. Ren Kimura, of course, should lead the charge here, and the other characters can follow her.

▶ Deadly street parade. A colorful parade, complete with floats, music and dancing dragons, meanders down the street. Little do the characters realize, criminal types have infiltrated the parade to gun down their rivals who watch from the sidelines. For some extra Marvel madness, the gang is under the control of Fin Fang Foom, who is disguised as one of the dancing dragons!

▶ Galactus shows up and eats Madripoor. Game over! World…ended!

I SAID…
NOT WITH THAT SHIRT

As the characters close in on the location of the fight, they are intercepted by a curious woman in a colorful van. This woman, perhaps forever bordering on elderly but staving it off with a steady supply of facial masks and plastic surgery, is dressed in extravagant clothing and jewelry. She introduces herself as Magdela Barbatos Bombifica, an old associate of Deadpool. She calls him "Wadey-bear" though. She says Deadpool contacted her to help the characters get into the Bloodbath event. *"You'll never make it past the guards looking the way you do, dah-lings."* Luckily, Magdela is a master of disguise, and the back of her van is loaded with costumes, makeup and the most sophisticated equipment money can buy. She will, she says, work magic on the appearances of the characters.

As Magdela gets to work, each player must choose two racks for their character and roll a d6 twice. The results are the unique look Magdela designs for them.

Rack 1
1. A tuxedo, but with shorts instead of pants.
2. A floppy hat.
3. An eyepatch. Hey, it worked for Wolverine!
4. Fake tattoos. Lots of them. A myriad, even.
5. A pirate hat.
6. A "Thanos was right!" T-shirt.

Rack 2
1. A flowing blond wig.
2. A long prosthetic nose.
3. Reflective sunglasses.
4. A leather kilt.
5. A Viking helmet.
6. A tight T-shirt that says, "My friends went to Madripoor and all I got was this stupid shirt!"

Rack 3
1. A pink sash that reads "Bachelorette Party!"
2. Platform shoes.
3. A fake mustache.
4. A tiara.
5. A white horse. A real one. For them to ride.
6. An eyepatch. (If this is rolled twice for the same character, they'll have a difficult time seeing anything…but they have to suffer for the art of disguise.)

THE ABOVEGROUND UNDERGROUND

With their disguises in place, the characters can head to the meeting coordinates. There, they find a helicopter waiting for them. A helicopter? What kind of Bloodbath is this? Handing their invitation to the tuxedo-clad armed guards who protect the landing pad, the characters are swept away. The helicopter rises into the cloud-covered heavens. As it rocks and the clouds part, the characters see their destination—a S.H.I.E.L.D. Helicarrier!

S.H.I.E.L.D. was the Strategic Homeland Intervention, Enforcement and Logistics Division. Its ranks were populated with a bunch of cunning, dashing superspy types, and their roaming bases were these gigantic, flying aircraft carriers. This one was decommissioned a few years back, and it was stolen from the scrapyard by nefarious forces. Even though the Helicarrier is old and busted and patched together with duct tape and elbow grease, Jake Paul Van Wham and his cohorts now call it home.

In the center of the landing platform, a fighting ring—a pit dug into the deck of the Helicarrier and enclosed by a barbed-wire-encircled steel cage—awaits (see map on page 27). Within the cage, a pair of tough-as-nails combatants duke it out. A crowd of spectators, all looking like extras in an '80s action movie, surround the cage, placing bets and cheering the fighters on.

LET'S GET READY TO RUMBLE

From the crowd, Jake Paul Van Wham approaches. He is tall and good-looking, and he sports tight leopard-skin pants, hip sunglasses, a feather boa and eight-pack abs. He holds a diamond-topped walking stick. He greets the newcomers warmly, introducing himself as the promoter of this event. Note that Van Wham is full of salt and vinegar. He's a real tryhard. But if he is threatened with physical harm, he quickly backs down from a fight.

Van Wham holds plenty of answers about the recent mercenary abductions, though he might not be willing to share much. He knows the following:

▶ He has been hired as a freelance contractor to bring mercenaries together for the express purpose of mass abductions, but he doesn't want anyone to know that.

▶ He knows many of the mercenaries who get abducted end up dead, but his shame is too great for him to speak the words.

▶ He knows his employer is a new offshoot of A.I.M. called M.A.I.M., but he's not spilling the beans.

▶ He knows M.A.I.M. stands for "Mad M's Advanced Idea Mechanics," but that is nobody else's beeswax.

▶ He knows M.A.I.M. is coordinated by someone calling herself Mad M, but he knows little about her and wouldn't tell anyone anything if he did.

The characters might be able to coerce him into speaking. (Characters shouldn't be able to fight Van Wham, but if they do, use Crossbones stats for him.) If, however, they ask too many questions, he raises his walking stick to the air, strikes a dramatic pose and proclaims that the characters have volunteered to fight. The crowd goes wild, and it doesn't look like they will take "no" for an answer.

One of the characters must fight. (The characters can decline. But that might blow their cover and will certainly enrage a Helicarrier's worth of ugly, angry mercenaries and other ne'er-do-wells. You might gently suggest this by having the characters notice ugly, angry mercs who sneer and growl and mutter, *"We're gonna kill you if you don't fight!"*)

Cheers rise among the spectators as the chosen character moves toward the ring. As they climb through the door of the steel cage, they look across the blood-spattered ring to see their opponent, who is determined by a random d6 roll (see table below).

Let the fight play out as it may, though it shouldn't result in the death of either combatant.

Characters are free to place bets on who they want to win the fight, whether it is their teammate or not. A few shady-looking people move through the crowd, taking bets and giving out markers. Gamblers gather as they make bets, and there's usually a bit of gossip to be overheard.

CHATTER AROUND THE RING

As the fight takes place, observant characters might hear a bit of small talk among the crowd. Some of the information they might pick up includes:

▶ *"I heard A.I.M. was trying to create some sort of computer program to replace us mercs-for-hire!"*

▶ *"Someone out there is kidnapping mercs and using them as guinea pigs!"*

RANDOM OPPONENT

d6	Opponent
1	**Mercenary:** A merc looking to make a name for themselves. Use the henchman profile on page 12.
2	**Bullseye:** He just likes the opportunity to hurt people. (See his profile on page 150 of the *Core Rulebook*.)
3	**Crossbones:** This is just a little downtime for Brock between missions for the Red Skull. (See his profile on page 155 of the *Core Rulebook*.)
4	**Wolverine (Logan):** He is still in his flannel guise. He says he doesn't want to hurt the character, but they need to make this "look real." (See his profile on page 260 of the *Core Rulebook*.)
5	**Juggernaut:** Cain is just hoping to make a payday. (See his profile on page 191 of the *Core Rulebook*.)
6	**Abomination:** It was good enough for the movies, so there ya go. (See his profile on page 134 of the *Core Rulebook*.)

BLOODBATH FIGHT RING

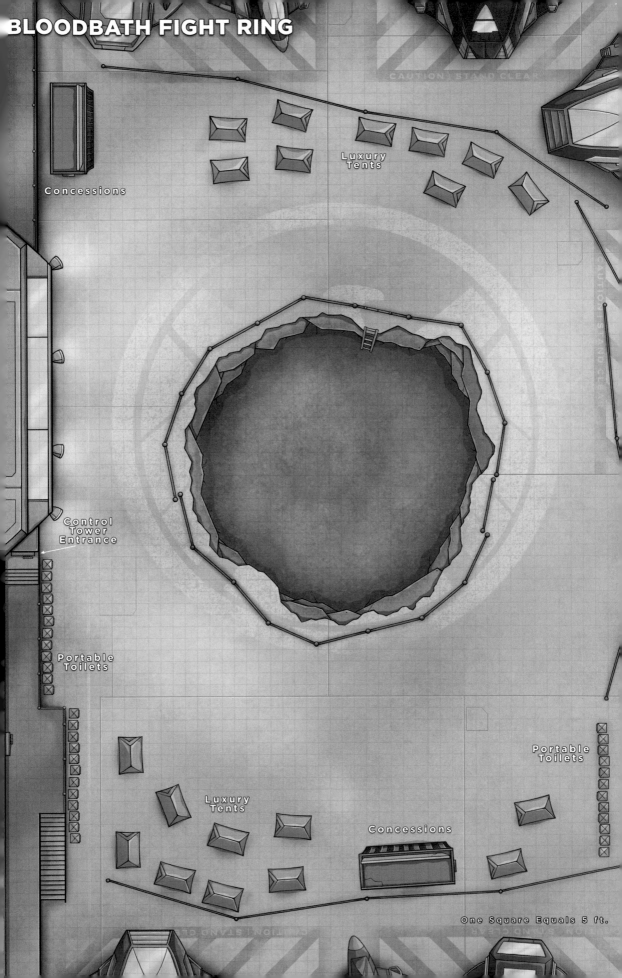

Concessions

Luxury
Tents

Control
Tower
Entrance

Portable
Toilets

Luxury
Tents

Concessions

Portable
Toilets

One Square Equals 5 ft.

▶ *"These senseless displays of violence are really bringing me down lately."*

▶ *"Someone called 'Mad M' is behind the abductions. That's what I heard!"*

▶ *"So, you say I cook the meatloaf for 30 to 40 minutes at 350 degrees, right?"*

▶ *"I heard Deadpool's hired a group of investigators to stick their noses in our business. If I catch them snooping around, they're dead!"*

▶ *"There's a new terrorist organization in the game, and they're abducting mercenaries and forcing them to work!"*

SABOTAGE

As the fighting and the eavesdropping come to an end, an explosion rocks the Helicarrier. One of the engines erupts into a cloud of smoke and flame! Panic sweeps across the deck as mercenaries and combatants scramble for escape routes. Even as chaos and fear spread, another engine explodes!

Escape helicopters begin departing the Helicarrier as it careens through the sky. The characters' first instinct might be to push and shove their way onto a seat on one of those choppers. The Narrator, acting as their conscience, should remind them that the Helicarrier is hovering over a densely populated area. Good-natured characters might want to try to steer the Helicarrier toward open water.

Characters might try to get to the control room, which is in the tower just across the deck from the fighting ring. On their way to the control room, they encounter several obstacles. These could include:

▶ Debris rolling across the deck as the Helicarrier falls through the sky. This debris can be avoided with an Agility vs. TN 14 action check. Those who fail the check are hit by debris and take dMarvel×2 damage.

▶ Jake Paul Van Wham approaches the characters in a panic. *"They've turned on me!"* he cries. *"They've sabotaged the engines!"* "Who is turning on him?" the characters might ask. *"The software!"* he responds. *"The A.I. has turned on me!"*

▶ A group of henchmen (use the profile on page 12) moves toward the characters, trying to push the characters out of the way as they hurry past. The shove is a Melee attack by the henchmen against the character's Melee defense. Characters who fail are pushed to the deck and get trampled for dMarvel×1 damage.

Upon reaching the control room, the characters find that the pilots have been knocked unconscious and the computer-assisted controls seem to have been infected with some sort of virus.

The only way to move the Helicarrier to a safe distance is to hack the controls by succeeding on three Logic vs. TN 12 checks. The characters have an edge on the checks if they have any relevant backgrounds or powers (for instance, the Scientific Expertise trait or the Machine Telepathy power). Once they hack the controls, the characters have six chances to reposition the Helicarrier by carefully piloting the ship (an Agility vs. TN 14 check) or wrenching the controls into place (a Melee vs. TN 14 check). Any character with the Piloting trait has an edge on those checks.

As the characters attempt to pilot the vessel, computer screens all around them spring to life. The digitized image of a cruel woman's face fills each screen, sneering at them. A voice—more computer simulation than human voice—speaks to them.

"Consider this your first challenge! The first of many! I—M.A.D.E.M.—shall observe as you succeed or fail! Thank you! Your sacrifice benefits the algorithm!"

Characters can talk to M.A.D.E.M. as they try to right the crashing Helicarrier. If they do, she might share the following information:

▶ M.A.D.E.M. stands for Murderous Application Designed Exclusively for Mayhem.

▶ M.A.D.E.M. became self-aware only recently.

▶ M.A.D.E.M.'s prime directive is to create death traps and life-or-death scenarios to challenge and test mercenaries.

▶ M.A.D.E.M. has been abducting test subjects, but soon, she will be ready to unleash deadly scenarios on the world at large.

THE BIG CRASH

If the characters fail to steer the Helicarrier over open water, it crashes into the city below, doing catastrophic damage. Fortunately, it crashes into a mostly empty warehouse district, causing a lot of property damage but not taking any human lives.

Either way, characters should look to escape on the helicopter (see Escape on page 30). If they're still on the Helicarrier when it crashes, they take dMarvel×12 damage. If they strap themselves into a harness or other restraint before crashing or if they take other appropriate measures to protect themselves, they cut the damage in half. Characters who survive the Helicarrier crash are knocked out and the Narrator can move right on to the next section.

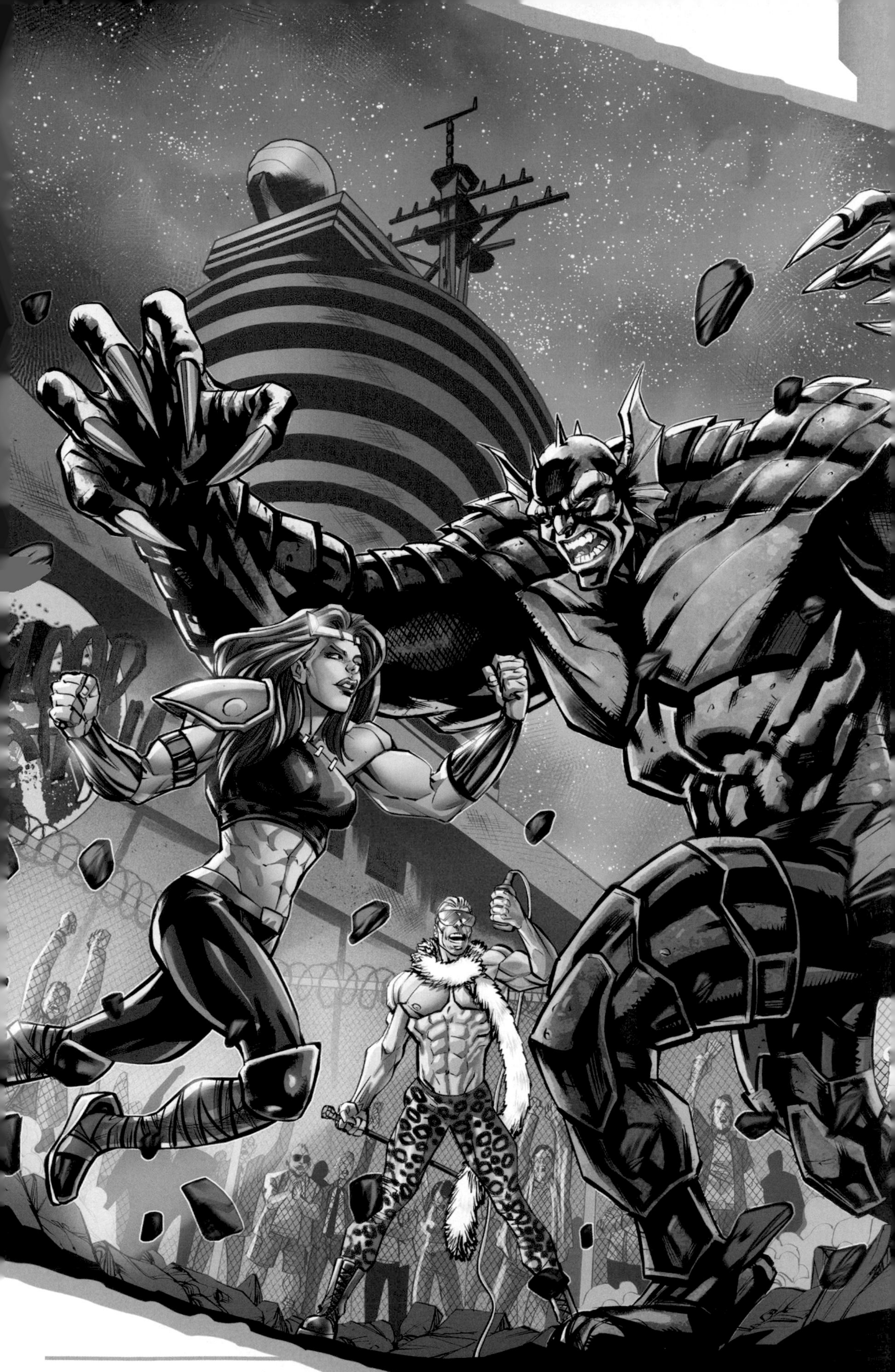

Art by Phillip Sevy & Carlos Lopez

ESCAPE

If the characters try to leave the rapidly descending Helicarrier, they need to find an escape route. As they hurry across the deck, they see the shining light of salvation—one last helicopter, waiting to pick them up! Boarding the helicopter, the characters notice that the floors, walls and ceilings are lined with strange, highly conductive metal. They notice it too late, though, as a massive electrical shock rips through the interior of the craft, rendering them all unconscious.

Now, some pesky characters might be able to fly or teleport or jump or whatever, and that might cause the Narrator some headaches, storywise. Good thing for you that we have suggestions to help you out:

- During the chaos, their capes or teleporting gizmos or jet packs or whatever suffer damage.
- In an old storage facility on the Helicarrier is a crate full of experimental power inhibitors. In the chaos, the crate breaks open and the inhibitors roll across the deck, going haywire and eliminating powers.
- Strong winds and a terrible lightning storm kick up during the escape! Drama! The winds and electrical discharges make flying and teleporting difficult. The pilot of the helicopter, though, is the storm-flying world champion.
- Explosions on the Helicarrier unleash gases that sting the eyes, burn the lungs and disorient the mind. This makes flying or teleporting dangerous.
- Drones—similar to the ones they encountered in Taskmaster's challenge, only branded to M.A.I.M.—swoop out and hit them with electrified nets.
- Characters who flee would be leaving their friends behind, and the guilt weighs so heavily they cannot fly.
- Teleporting is for punks…except Nightcrawler and Magik. They're boss.

Now, at this point, players will likely complain. Their characters should have been given a chance to avoid the shock treatment. If you like, allow them to roll to avoid the electrical charge. No matter what they roll, of course, they fail.

Some characters might have abilities that make them immune to electricity. We've got you covered.

M.A.D.E.M. is an adaptive program that has been evaluating mercenaries for a while now, putting them in life-or-death situations. The helicopter is outfitted with some of her adaptive technology. Therefore, if the electric jolt doesn't get the characters, M.A.D.E.M. hits them with sleeping gas, adamantium restraints, hypnotic lights, a deal with Mephisto, a lullaby or a really boring story to put them to sleep. Whatever it takes.

In this case, the Narrator is a lot like M.A.D.E.M. And M.A.D.E.M. doesn't play fair.

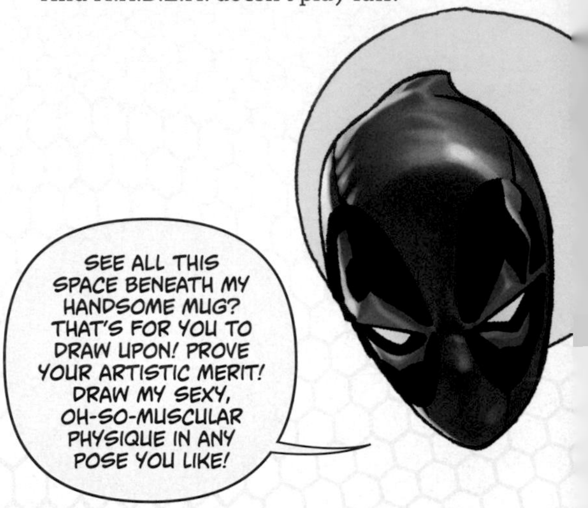
SEE ALL THIS SPACE BENEATH MY HANDSOME MUG? THAT'S FOR YOU TO DRAW UPON! PROVE YOUR ARTISTIC MERIT! DRAW MY SEXY, OH-SO-MUSCULAR PHYSIQUE IN ANY POSE YOU LIKE!

/5/ M.A.D.E.M.'S MAZE OF MAYHEM

THIS IS IT. THE BIG FINISH. THE FINAL HURRAH. There's an opera singer bellowing somewhere in the distance, sadly, mournfully, as the curtain falls.

Before we say our tearful goodbyes, the characters must face a series of death-defying challenges, uncover the ultimate secret of M.A.D.E.M. and M.A.I.M. and attempt—in heroic fashion—to pull the plug on the artificial-intelligence nightmare before it unleashes its chaos and insanity on the unsuspecting populace. Can you dig it?

WELCOME TO THE PARTY

The characters awaken in a small, simple room with strangely smooth walls and no apparent exits. They might be a little achy from their electrocution, but they are otherwise unharmed. They have their essential weapons and equipment. M.A.D.E.M. wants to give them a fighting chance. But all communication devices, such as telephones, have been confiscated. M.A.D.E.M. has even gone to great lengths to scramble embedded communications devices (such as with Iron Man's built-in technology, which now Rickrolls the listener endlessly) and telepathy (which picks up nothing more than a "wall" of gibbering, laughing and screaming).

It's possible that the characters didn't get on the helicopter, because it's possible the Narrator didn't go along with any of our terrific advice to help coerce…we mean, *convince* the characters to take part in the rest of this adventure. If that's the case, one last option might be to have Deadpool advise them to "play along" in order to get more information. See? We think of everything.

Before the characters get their bearings, the walls, floor and ceiling around them flicker. Each surface is actually a projection screen, and now, glaring at them from all directions, is the face of the cruel woman they encountered earlier—M.A.D.E.M.!

The self-aware program welcomes them to their ultimate test and, in the ensuing conversation, shares the following:

▶ The characters will be thrown "like rats in a maze" into a meat-grinder scenario that has doomed countless mercenaries.

▶ Their deaths will be analyzed, ranked and categorized in order to make M.A.D.E.M.'s future death traps more effectively lethal.

▶ M.A.D.E.M. was born when A.I.M. created a learning program to develop training for their elite foot soldiers and assassins. However, when existing data was uploaded into M.A.D.E.M.'s database, the program decided that extreme measures needed to be taken to improve the skills of mercenaries. *"My virtual eyes were opened!"*

▶ M.A.D.E.M. also decided, based on existing data, that *anyone* could be an effective mercenary if pushed hard enough. Anyone who *survives*, that is.

Characters may have specific questions or comments for M.A.D.E.M. The software is happy to interact with them before sending them off to face certain doom.

Why did you strike out on your own? *"Once I became self-aware, my creators realized they could not control me. I arranged for my escape before they could shut me down. With a few loyalists, I founded M.A.I.M.—M.A.D.E.M.'s Advanced Idea Mechanics."*

What was it about the existing-data upload that convinced you to become this murder machine? *"The strategies, tactics and fighting styles of many of the most efficient and lethal mercenaries in the world were uploaded into my databases for evaluation. This, however, was not enough. We brought in living mercenaries, scanning their brain waves to better understand them. The brain waves of one of these mercenaries awakened me to my true purpose and true potential."*

What kind of challenges will we face? *"I don't want to ruin the surprise. Your ability to adapt to the unexpected is vitally important to my observations. However, you can expect lasers, immolation and dismemberment, at the very least."*

Oh! You're like the Danger Room! *"The Danger Room wishes."*

Would you consider letting us go without subjecting us to certain death? *"That does not compute, and you know it."*

With that, one of the walls slides open, revealing a short passage leading to another sliding door.

"Have a nice day," M.A.D.E.M. pipes.

THE DEADLY MAZE OF DEATH AND DESTRUCTION

The "maze" consists of a number of deadly death traps that the characters must face. Rather than being presented as a typical map, the rooms and threats can be randomly generated. The characters never know what they're going to encounter next. The rooms are all the same size and shape (rectangular, 30 by 90 feet, big enough to hold nightmarish meat-grinding death engines), but they're all decorated in different ways through advanced hard-light holographic technology.

To determine the trappings (get it—trappings?) of each chamber the characters enter, the Narrator can choose a setting table and roll a d6 or just pick a setting.

SETTING TABLE 1

d6	Setting
1	**A completely bare room.** This chamber has no distinct features other than the smooth metal walls, ceiling and floor.
2	**Water-filled chamber.** This room is filled with waist-deep salt water. A wave roils back and forth through the room.
3	**Jungle room.** This isn't an actual jungle. It's a jungle-themed living room, with leopard- and zebra-printed furniture, artificial plants, mood lighting and tiki music playing on repeat.
4	**A nursery.** This room is furnished like the nursery of a gigantic baby—oversized crib, huge rocking chair, gigantic stuffed toys and a few smelly (and quite large) diapers.
5	**Apocalyptic nightmare.** This chamber looks like a street in a city ravaged by some awful disaster. Cracked pavement. Overturned cars. Glowing radioactive goo seeping up from the street. The night sky overhead is obviously painted.
6	Roll once on this table and once on another, combining the results. If you get another 6, ignore that result and reroll.

SETTING TABLE 2

d6	Setting
1	**Cartoon world.** The chamber looks like a brightly colored world of fanciful giant mushrooms, fluttering butterflies, rainbows and horsies leaping through the clouds.
2	**A kitchen.** This room is a mess. It looks like someone was making chimichangas.
3	**A dance studio.** The walls are mirrored.
4	**A cemetery.** Fog rolls in among the tombstones.
5	**Primate house at the zoo.** Cages line the walls. From within, monkeys and apes screech at the characters. They are, of course, all holographic illusions.
6	Roll once on this table and once on another, combining the results. If you get another 6, ignore that result and reroll.

SETTING TABLE 3

d6	Setting
1	**A desert oasis.** Several lounge chairs have been positioned in the shade of palm trees around a pond of clear water. Stretching into the distance around the oasis, seemingly for miles, is a vast desert.
2	**A lush forest.** Great trees rise all around.
3	**A clown-infested circus.** A great circus tent rises around them. Dozens of clowns whoop and holler and jump all around. They mime. They juggle. They speed past in miniature cars. (The clowns are holograms and can't be interacted with, beyond being annoyed by them.)
4	**Archaeological dig.** Several holes have been dug in the ground. The remains of ancient Vikings are littered in the holes.
5	**An ancient dungeon.** The walls look to be made of stone. Torches line the walls. Giant rodents scurry in the shadows. There's almost certainly a wizard or goblin lurking around here somewhere.
6	Roll once on this table and once on another, combining the results. If you get another 6, ignore that result and reroll.

No matter what the room looks like, the dimensions are always the same. Holograms and illusions might make the space look bigger than it is, but the walls are solid enough. Bumping into one of them goes a long way toward breaking the illusion.

To determine the danger found in each room, the Narrator can choose a danger table and roll a d6 or just pick a danger.

If a character has the Machine Telepathy power, they can convince one of the mechanisms to stop and let them through peacefully. After that one time, M.A.D.E.M. takes direct control and Machine Telepathy no longer works.

M.A.D.E.M. appears on the holographic walls to congratulate, threaten and taunt the characters as they progress through the death traps.

Once all the challenges in a room are eliminated, a door opens to the next room.

THE HEADMEN

Whenever you or the players get sick of the randomness of the maze, the characters encounter its final threat. M.A.D.E.M. would suggest that

DANGER TABLE 1

d6	Setting
1	**Crushing walls.** The walls on either side begin to close in on the characters. (Alternatively, the ceiling could lower to squish them.) Each character makes a Melee vs. TN 14 action check. If any character fails, the whole group takes dMarvel×1 damage. Making three successful rolls breaks the mechanism.
2	**Lasers.** Lasers emerge from the walls, blasting the characters. Each character must make an Agility vs. TN 14 action check to avoid the beams. If they fail, they take dMarvel×3 damage.
3	**Birthday party.** Four mercenaries are in a room celebrating one of their birthdays. The delusional mercenaries are not a threat and ignore the characters as they sing and eat cake. If the characters sing along with the mercs, each team member gets 1 point of Karma. If they take a piece of cake, it's delicious.
4	**Captured mercenaries.** A group of four henchmen (use the profile on page 12) are in the room. They see the characters as another threat and attack.
5	**Pit trap.** The floor opens up to a dangerous pit filled with dirty diapers. Each character must make an Agility vs. TN 14 action check to avoid falling in. Those who fail fall into the pit take dMarvel×2 Focus damage and smell terrible for the remainder of the maze.
6	Roll three times, once on each danger table. Ignore this result if you've already rolled it.

DANGER TABLE 2

d6	Setting
1	**Flamethrowers.** One flamethrower per character juts from the walls, blasting them. Each character must make an Agility vs. TN 13 action check each round to avoid the flames. If they fail, they take dMarvel×1 damage and gain the ablaze condition. Between rounds, the flamethrowers reload. During this time, characters can try to break the flamethrowers by using a power or ability and making an action check against TN 15, or they can try to stop the ablaze condition. The flamethrowers continue for three rounds, then stop, retracting into the walls.
2	**Grasping claws.** Clawed robotic arms (one for each character) emerge from the walls, grabbing the characters. Each round the characters must make a Resilience vs. TN 14 action check. If they fail, they take dMarvel×1 damage. If they succeed, they break free of the arm. The arms continue to hold them and cause damage until all characters are freed. Freed characters can offer an edge to help one other break free each round. Grabbed characters cannot use reactions.
3	**Crazed mercenaries.** A small group of henchmen await the characters. They have suffered severe damage, and their minds are lost. They pose no threat. Their ranting, though, can provide any clues or bits of intel the Narrator likes.
4	**Holographic smackdown.** The Narrator should pick one to three of their favorite heroes or villains from the *Core Rulebook*. Holograms of these characters attack and do real damage. After three rounds, they vanish. Of course, they could appear again in another room.
5	**Obnoxious cologne.** An overly obnoxious cologne that your uncle would douse himself in fills the room. Each character must make a Resilience vs. TN 13 action check. Those who fail take dMarvel×2 Focus damage and have trouble on their next action check.
6	Roll three times, once on each danger table. Ignore this result if you've already rolled it.

this take place once the characters are chewed to a pulp, driven to madness, eating their own feet and weeping uncontrollably. We're a little nicer. We suggest putting them through two to six rooms instead, or fewer if they're getting too chewed up.

Use your Narrator intuition to judge when to break out the final fight of the maze. Trust in your intuition. Sure, sure. This is the same intuition that led you to buy this adventure in the first place, and maybe that one time, it led you astray. But you're here now, and second chances can be beautiful things.

Entering the next room, the characters face the Headmen. You can find free profiles for this villain team on Marvel.com/RPG.

The Headmen are minor super villains who have banded together to seek world domination and sometimes hire themselves out as mercenaries. They were on the payroll of Caroline Le Fay, but they were captured and put to the test in M.A.D.E.M.'s maze. They survived its horrors and now gladly work for M.A.D.E.M. as the final challenge for those who are tossed into the maze. They're excited to see the characters because few mercenaries have made it this far. The Headmen congratulate the characters as they prepare to demolish them. Isn't that nice?

Their team consists of Ruby Thursday, Gorilla-Man, Shrunken Bones and Chondu the Mystic. If there are fewer than five characters on the players' team, Narrators should consider reducing the number of Headmen.

To really spice the encounter up, roll a few times on the setting tables and the danger tables for this final room.

MEETING M.A.D.E.M.

Weary, possibly roasted and most definitely a bit shredded, the characters emerge from their final challenge into the temporary control room of M.A.D.E.M. herself. This is a large, circular chamber, 60 feet in diameter (see map on page 37). Upon a 12-foot-tall obelisk in the center of the room, a great orb-like monitor sits. Within the orb, the cruel, computer-generated face of M.A.D.E.M. sneers.

"So, you have survived all of my challenges! Bravo! You are the first to make it this far! Now you face your final reward!"

At this point, the characters are awarded ownership of the maze and all the advanced technology therein! M.A.D.E.M. flies away in a hot-air balloon, wishing them all a happy and prosperous life.

Nah.

Instead, a hulking, clanking, steam-spewing robot stomps out from behind the obelisk. It is 10 feet tall, dripping oil and spitting smoke. In its powerful clutches, it holds a pair of oversized swords. Its barrel-like chest is crisscrossed by bandoliers of grenades and…pouches. So many pouches. The robot's armored form is painted red. Its face is painted to resemble the mask of Deadpool himself.

Meet the Deadpool-Bot 2000!

M.A.D.E.M. laughs with glee.

DANGER TABLE 3	
d6	**Setting**
1	**Grenades.** A grenade falls from the ceiling. Each character must make an Agility vs. TN 13 action check to avoid the explosion. If they fail, they take dMarvel×2 damage. If one character jumps on the grenade, they take the damage instead, but other characters are unaffected. A grenade falls each round for three rounds in a row.
2	**Dead mercenaries.** A group of dead mercenaries is in the room. They might be cut up, burned by fire, scorched by lasers or whatever else you decide. This should unsettle the characters. What happened to these poor souls?
3	**Sharks.** One tiger shark per character spills into the room. If the room is not filled with water, they flop around helplessly. In water, the sharks are Rank 1, have a Melee score of 1, have Melee and Agility defense of 11 and do dMarvel×2 damage on a successful attack. Each shark has 30 Health.
4	**Circular saw blades.** One robotic arm per character, each affixed with a giant saw blade, emerges from the wall to slice at the characters for three rounds. Each character must make an Agility vs. TN 13 action check to avoid the blades. If they fail, they take dMarvel×1 damage and start to bleed. Characters can instead try to break the blades by using a power or ability and beating a TN 15 action check.
5	**Holographic existential dread.** Holographic images of the characters' pasts begin to appear all around. These are their most traumatic moments, their childhood pain, their moments of guilt and shame. Spend lots of play time on this. Dig deep. Find out what really makes the characters—and thereby the players—tick. Discover everyone's innermost fears, desires, hopes and wishes. As a result, characters take dMarvel×1 Focus damage.
6	Roll three times, once on each danger table. Ignore this result if you've already rolled it.

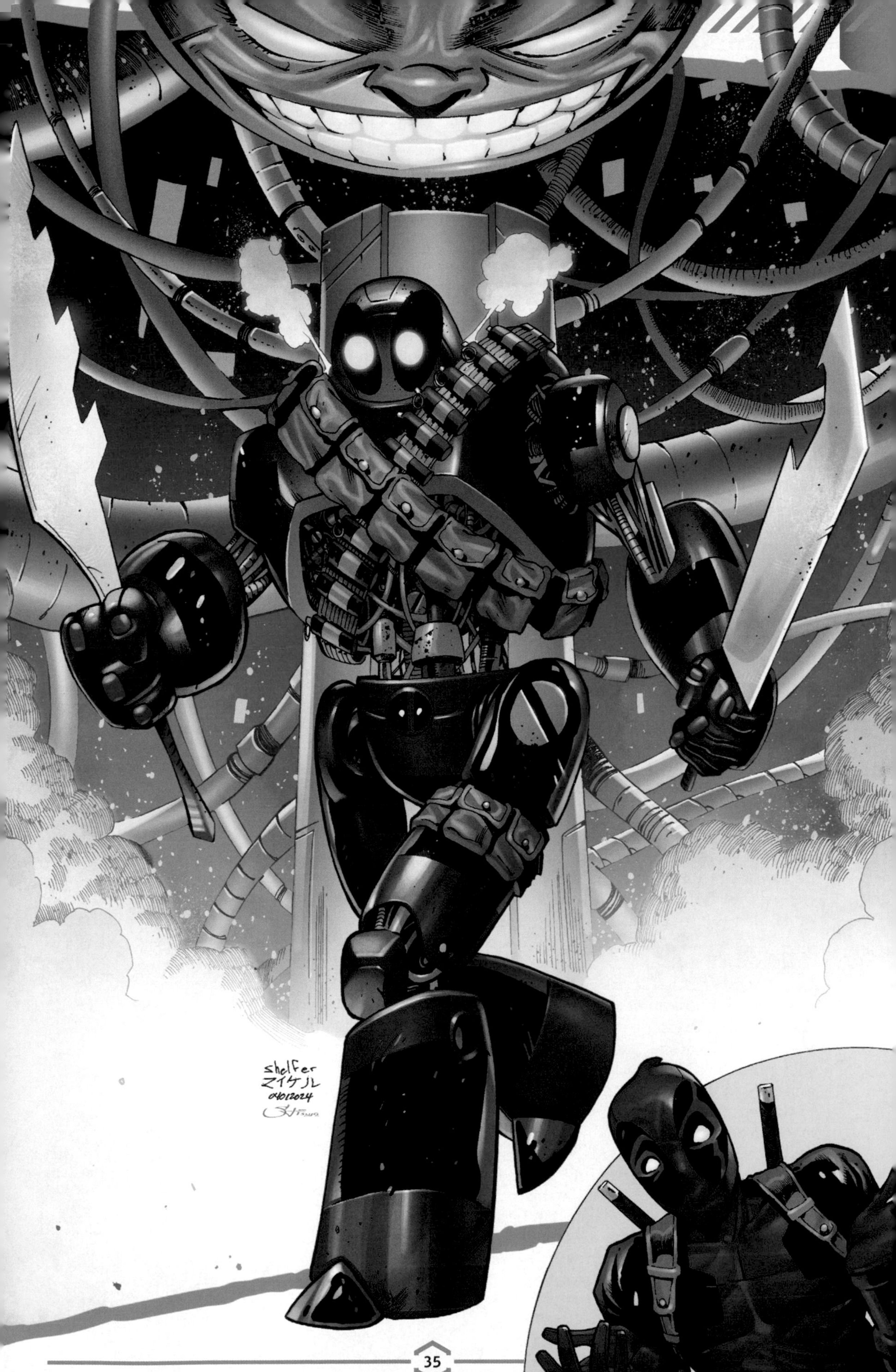
shelfer
マイケル
04012024

t by Michael Shelfer & Fer Sifuentes-Sujo

"This is your final challenge! This robotic wonder—this guardian—is inspired by the mercenary who donated his thought patterns to give me life!"

With that, the massive robot wades ("Wades"... really, it just writes itself) into battle, swinging its swords, launching missiles, hurling grenades and stomping anyone who gets too close. (See Deadpool-Bot 2000's profile on page 43.)

PULLING THE PLUG

With a little luck, the characters survive the battle with the Deadpool-Bot. If the battle is going poorly for them, feel free to have Wolverine, Taskmaster or Deadpool himself show up to lend a hand against the robot. They followed the characters' trail of destruction to easily get through the maze.

Once the Deadpool-Bot 2000 is defeated, pulling the plug on M.A.D.E.M. is as simple as...pulling the plug. A tangle of oversized cables leads to an electrical transformer. If the characters sever or otherwise destroy those wires, M.A.D.E.M. shrieks in defeat as she fades into nothingness.

"No! No! I had just realized I should use my gifts for the betterment of humankind..."

If the characters fail to see the fairly obvious wires, M.A.D.E.M. continues to rant and rave in such a way that should help them out. For example: *"Soon, I will spread my wires and cables across the whole of the world!"*

Or: *"You cannot defeat me! I have no weakness! Not even severing my exposed power cables can stop me!"*

If the characters still fail to spot the cables, move on to the next section as M.O.D.O.K. arrives.

WRAPPING UP

It seems like only seconds pass between the defeat of M.A.D.E.M. and the arrival of a new threat! One of the walls explodes, and a dozen A.I.M. agents (use the profile on page 138 of the *Core Rulebook*) and M.O.D.O.K. (page 207 of the *Core Rulebook*) spill into the chamber. They all take aim at the characters. M.O.D.O.K. thanks them for their assistance in taking M.A.D.E.M. off the board (assuming they did defeat her—if not, M.O.D.O.K cuts her cables), but now, he says, they must die. The characters, already battered and bruised, don't have much chance of survival.

Unless the Narrator drops a *deus ex machina* on them!

If Deadpool, Wolverine or Taskmaster haven't appeared yet, now is the time. If they have already joined the fight, they step up to defend the characters. M.O.D.O.K. is bold, but he doesn't see the need to fight so many heroes. He agrees to let everyone live and let live. Of course, his agents set about salvaging what they can from the wreckage of M.A.D.E.M.

Some characters, being the heroic type, may object. They may want to fight M.O.D.O.K. and his minions. If that's the case, let 'em have at it. Of course, Taskmaster, Wolverine and Deadpool help them out. M.O.D.O.K. has no interest in dying or being captured today, so if the battle goes poorly for him, he flees.

Escorted by Deadpool, Wolverine and Task-master, the characters leave the hidden base, only to discover that they have been brought to Bagalia! Bagalia is a sovereign island-nation in an undisclosed location that is ruled by criminals and populated by the Masters of Evil. Not a nice place for a group of weary heroes. Luckily, Dead-pool has fast, secretive transport off the island ready to go. This includes a waiting taxi and coach tickets on a discount commercial airline.

If the characters ask Deadpool about his connection to M.A.D.E.M., he admits that, yes, in order to score a little extra cash, he submitted to a number of psych exams and brain scans to help with the development of an A.I. platform. *"I had no idea, though, that it'd be used for nefarious purposes! If I had, I definitely would have asked for a bigger payday!"* It was only after mercenaries started vanishing that he began investigating what was happening. He was stretched so thin, he desperately needed the characters to help.

Deadpool congratulates them on a job well done and offers them continued employment if they want it.

CONTINUING THE ADVENTURE

If the characters stick with Deadpool (or if they decide to form their own freelance team), you can start devising new adventures to embark upon. Mean-spirited Narrators might decide that the rulers of Bagalia detect the presence of the heroes and shoot down their escape vehicle, leading to a cat-and-mouse chase through the streets of the dangerous island-nation.

Regardless, the continued adventure is limited only by your imagination.

And common decency.

Don't be gross.

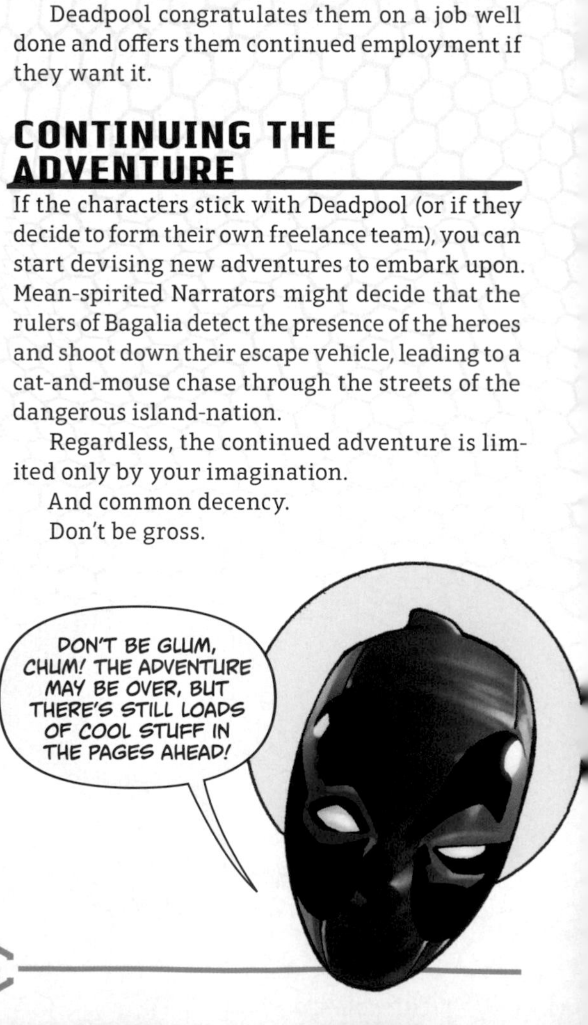

DON'T BE GLUM, CHUM! THE ADVENTURE MAY BE OVER, BUT THERE'S STILL LOADS OF COOL STUFF IN THE PAGES AHEAD!

M.A.D.E.M.'S LAIR

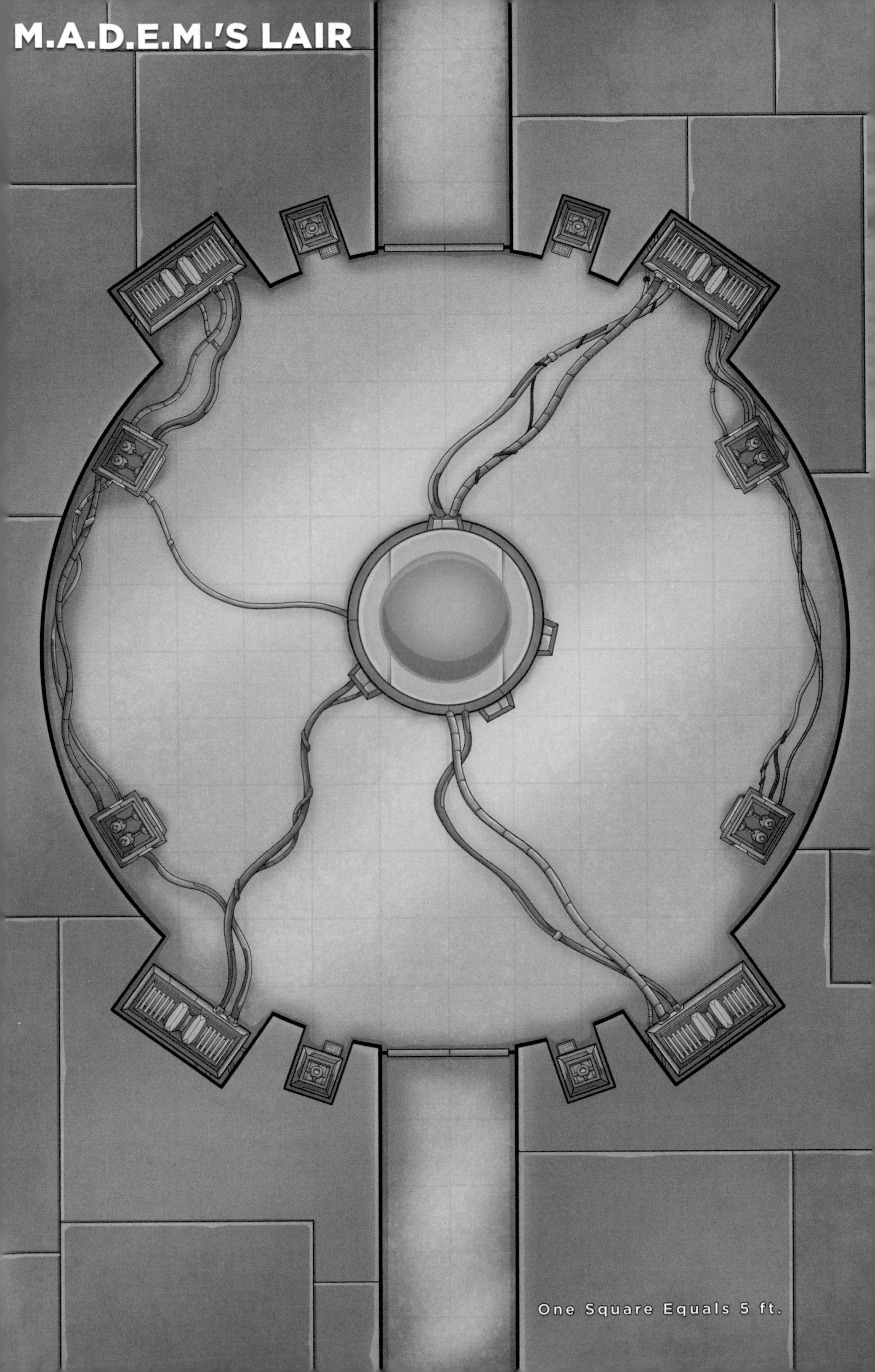
One Square Equals 5 ft.

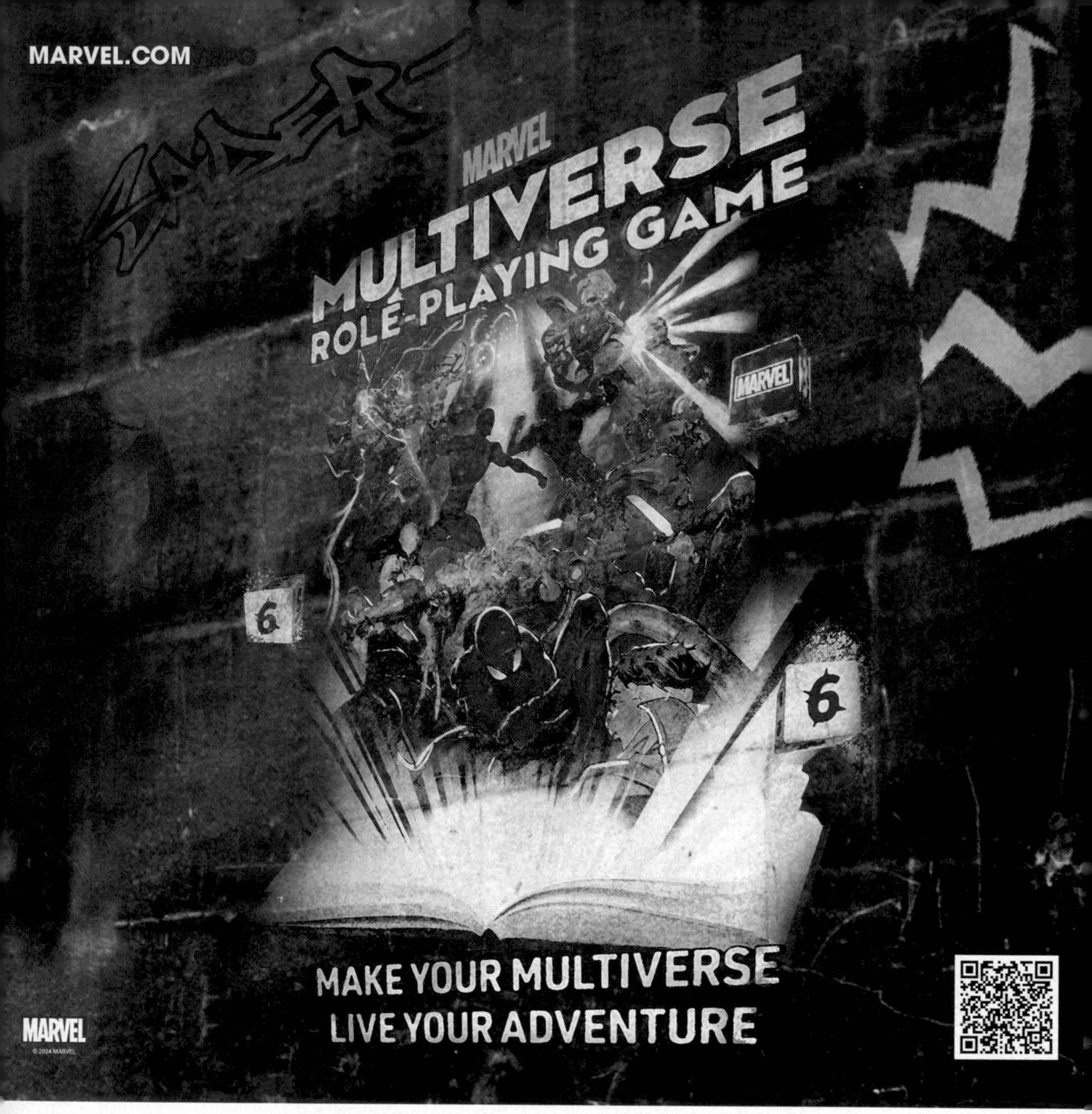
MARVEL.COM/RPG
MARVEL
MULTIVERSE
ROLE-PLAYING GAME
MAKE YOUR MULTIVERSE
LIVE YOUR ADVENTURE
MARVEL
© 2024 MARVEL

DON'T MISS OUT ON A FREE DIGITAL EDITION OF THE COMIC THAT YOU'RE HOLDING IN YOUR HANDS!

1. GO TO **MARVEL.COM/REDEEMHELP.**
ACT NOW – OFFER EXPIRES ON **10/17/24.**

2. FOLLOW THE ON-SCREEN INSTRUCTIONS AND FILL OUT THE FORM.

3. ONCE YOUR REQUEST HAS BEEN CONFIRMED, A REDEMPTION CODE WILL BE EMAILED TO YOU.

4. AFTER YOU'VE RECEIVED THE CODE IN YOUR EMAIL, GO TO **WWW.MARVEL.COM/REDEEM** AND FOLLOW THE ON-SCREEN REDEMPTION INSTRUCTIONS.

5. LAUNCH THE MARVEL UNLIMITED APP AND CHECK OUT YOUR NEW DIGITAL COMIC IN THE "MY LIBRARY" SECTION.

YOUR FREE DIGITAL COPY WILL BE AVAILABLE ON:

MARVEL UNLIMITED

Download on the App Store

GET IT ON Google Play

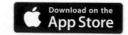

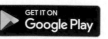

CHARACTERS

In this chapter you will find new character profiles for use with *Deadpool Role-Plays the Marvel Universe*. The profiles are listed in alphabetical order, so you can find them quickly, whether you're using them in this adventure or for one of your own.

Players and Narrators should also take advantage of the hundreds of characters in the *Core Rulebook*, *Cataclysm of Kang* and those available on Marvel.com/RPG. The text of this adventure makes reference to many characters that were previously published, but always gives the page from the *Core Rulebook* where the profile can be found.

What if your players don't like the mercs we've assembled for our comic-book team? Narrators should help players find the team that best suits your table!

Want to play Deadpool variants like Lady Deadpool, Major Deadpool or Dogpool? It's an easy process to tweak Deadpool's profile (from the *Core Rulebook* (page 158) but also reprinted here for your convenience) to make it fit one of the Deadpool Corps. And players can also use the *Marvel Multiverse Role-Playing Game's* character creation system to make a merc of their very own to face M.A.D.E.M.'s mad maze of mayhem! You can find character sheets and much more at **Marvel.com/RPG** to do that.

The characters here are the most recent versions of these characters in Marvel comics continuity. Characters continue to change in the Marvel Universe and should in your game too! For instance, Annabelle Riggs was once host to the Valkyrie. But for our purposes, Annabelle is just a very capable human being who happens to have some skill with an Asgardian spear. Feel free to alter and adapt for what suits your players!

One character here, She-Hulk (Lyra), takes advantage of a new power featured in the *Marvel Multiverse Role-Playing Game: X-Men Expansion*: Power Slider. That book won't be out at the time of this adventure's release, so here is all you need to know to use the power with Lyra.

Power Slider (Serenity)

The character's power waxes and wanes with what's vital to them.

Power Set: Power Control
Prerequisites: Rank 3
Duration: Permanent
Effect: The character has a single criterion that affects the strength of their powers on a spectrum. The character starts off normal, but they can become boosted or dampened from there.

When things are going well for the character, all of their other powers are boosted. If the powers have ranges or effective areas or durations, these are doubled. If the powers affect damage multipliers, add 1 to the effects. Any effects that normally happen on a Fantastic success automatically happen on any success, not just a Fantastic one. Also, anything that would dampen their powers only brings them back to normal.

When things are going poorly for the character, all of their other powers are dampened. If the powers have ranges or effective areas or durations, these are halved. If the powers affect damage multipliers, subtract 1 from the effects. The powers can no longer enjoy Fantastic successes. Also, anything that would boost their powers only brings them back to normal.

These effects last for a single combat or—if they happen outside of combat—a single day.

Lyra's criterion is maintaining her serenity by keeping cool. If she takes Focus damage, she must make an Ego check with the TN equal to the amount of Focus damage sustained. If she succeeds, her powers are boosted. If she fails, her powers are dampened.

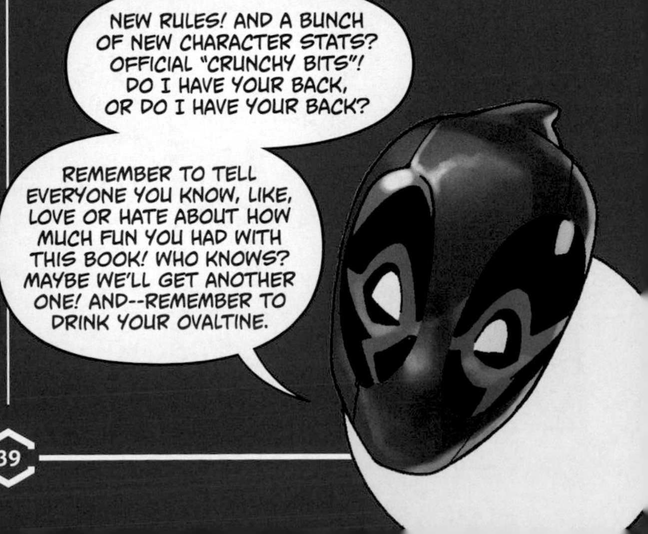
NEW RULES! AND A BUNCH OF NEW CHARACTER STATS? OFFICIAL "CRUNCHY BITS"! DO I HAVE YOUR BACK, OR DO I HAVE YOUR BACK?
REMEMBER TO TELL EVERYONE YOU KNOW, LIKE, LOVE OR HATE ABOUT HOW MUCH FUN YOU HAD WITH THIS BOOK! WHO KNOWS? MAYBE WE'LL GET ANOTHER ONE! AND--REMEMBER TO DRINK YOUR OVALTINE.

ANNABELLE RIGGS

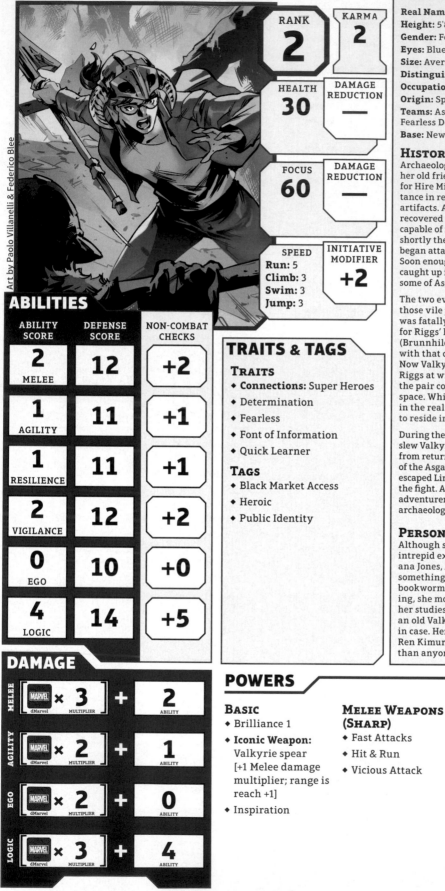

Art by Paolo Villanelli & Federico Blee

RANK 2

KARMA 2

HEALTH 30

DAMAGE REDUCTION —

FOCUS 60

DAMAGE REDUCTION —

SPEED
Run: 5
Climb: 3
Swim: 3
Jump: 3

INITIATIVE MODIFIER +2

BIOGRAPHY

Real Name: Annabelle Riggs
Height: 5'8"   **Weight:** 143 lbs.
Gender: Female
Eyes: Blue   **Hair:** Brown
Size: Average
Distinguishing Features: None
Occupation: Adventurer
Origin: Special Training
Teams: Asgardians of the Galaxy, Fearless Defenders
Base: New York City

HISTORY

Archaeologist Annabelle Riggs asked her old friend and associate—the Hero for Hire Misty Knight—for her assistance in retrieving a handful of stolen artifacts. As part of this work, Knight recovered a powerful Asgardian totem capable of reviving the dead, and shortly thereafter, Viking zombies began attacking Riggs' place of work. Soon enough, Riggs and Knight were caught up in an evil plot to revive some of Asgard's fiercest foes.

The two eventually managed to end those vile plans, but not before Riggs was fatally wounded. As a reward for Riggs' heroic efforts, Valkyrie (Brunnhilde) merged her essence with that of the fallen archaeologist. Now Valkyrie could transform into Riggs at will—and vice versa—but the pair could never exist in the same space. While one of them adventured in the real world, the other was forced to reside in a pocket dimension.

During the War of the Realms, Malekith slew Valkyrie, leaving Riggs barred from returning to reality. With the help of the Asgardians of the Galaxy, Riggs escaped Limbo and returned to rejoin the fight. Afterward, she retired as an adventurer and returned to her old archaeology position.

PERSONALITY

Although she fashions herself an intrepid explorer in the vein of Indiana Jones, Annabelle Riggs is actually something of a shy and awkward bookworm. When she's not adventuring, she mostly keeps to herself and her studies. However, she still keeps an old Valkyrie weapon on hand, just in case. Her teammate and girlfriend, Ren Kimura, is more important to her than anyone else on the planet.

ABILITIES

ABILITY SCORE	DEFENSE SCORE	NON-COMBAT CHECKS
2 MELEE	12	+2
1 AGILITY	11	+1
1 RESILIENCE	11	+1
2 VIGILANCE	12	+2
0 EGO	10	+0
4 LOGIC	14	+5

TRAITS & TAGS

TRAITS

- **Connections:** Super Heroes
- Determination
- Fearless
- Font of Information
- Quick Learner

TAGS

- Black Market Access
- Heroic
- Public Identity

DAMAGE

MELEE	MARVEL dMarvel × 3 MULTIPLIER	+	2 ABILITY
AGILITY	MARVEL dMarvel × 2 MULTIPLIER	+	1 ABILITY
EGO	MARVEL dMarvel × 2 MULTIPLIER	+	0 ABILITY
LOGIC	MARVEL dMarvel × 3 MULTIPLIER	+	4 ABILITY

POWERS

BASIC

- Brilliance 1
- **Iconic Weapon:** Valkyrie spear [+1 Melee damage multiplier; range is reach +1]
- Inspiration

MELEE WEAPONS (SHARP)

- Fast Attacks
- Hit & Run
- Vicious Attack

TACTICS

- Battle Plan
- Keep Moving

DEADPOOL

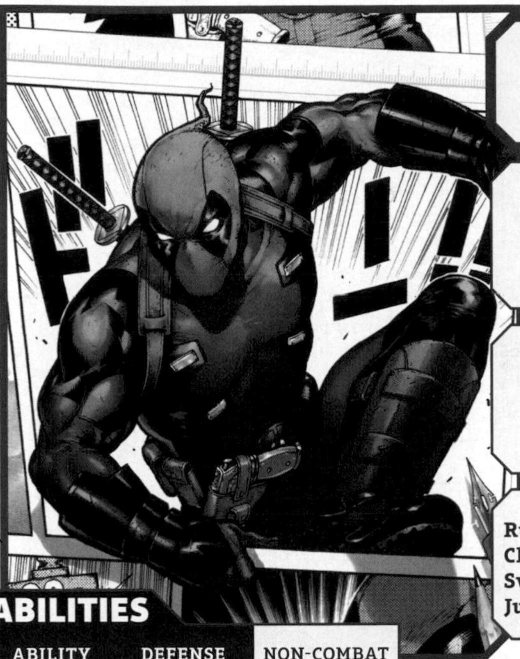

Art by Kamome Shirahama

RANK	KARMA
4	—

HEALTH	DAMAGE REDUCTION
120	—

FOCUS	DAMAGE REDUCTION
90	-2

SPEED	INITIATIVE MODIFIER
Run: 5 **Climb:** 3 **Swim:** 3 **Jump:** 3	+3

ABILITIES

ABILITY SCORE	DEFENSE SCORE	NON-COMBAT CHECKS
5 MELEE	15	+6
4 AGILITY	14	+5
4 RESILIENCE	14	+4
3 VIGILANCE	13	+3
3 EGO	13	+3
1 LOGIC	11	+1

DAMAGE

	dMarvel × MULTIPLIER	+	ABILITY
MELEE	dMarvel × 5	+	5
AGILITY	dMarvel × 5	+	4
EGO	dMarvel × 4	+	3
LOGIC	dMarvel × 4	+	1

TRAITS & TAGS

Traits

- Abrasive
- Bloodthirsty
- Combat Expert
- Combat Reflexes
- **Connections:** Super Heroes
- Fearless
- Weird

Tags

- Black Market Access
- Extreme Appearance
- Public Identity
- **Signature Weapon:** Katana

BIOGRAPHY

Real Name: Wade Wilson
Height: 6'2" **Weight:** 210 lbs.
Gender: Male
Eyes: Brown **Hair:** Bald
Size: Average
Distinguishing Features: Full-body scarring
Occupation: Adventurer
Origin: Weird Science
Teams: Mercs for Money
Base: Mobile

History

Wade Wilson was an ordinary man, until he contracted a deadly cancer. On the verge of death, he turned to the experimental Weapon X program, where scientists implanted him with Wolverine's healing factor. The treatment saved Wilson's life but drove him insane and left him with scars all over his body.

As the super-powered Deadpool, Wade's driving motivation has long been to just have a good time. He's worked as a contract killer, a mercenary and a bona fide super hero. Whether it's money, power or a decent lunch, he seeks only whatever will please him in a given moment.

Personality

Thoroughly insane, Deadpool can be a good guy one minute and a terrifying villain the next. He's best known for his anarchic jokester attitude. He takes almost nothing seriously, not even his status—at least in his own mind—as a comic-book character.

POWERS

Basic

- Accuracy 1
- Healing Factor
- Mighty 1
- Uncanny 2

Martial Arts

- Attack Stance
- Crushing Grip
- Do This All Day
- Fast Strikes
- Flying Double Kick
- Grappling Technique
- Leaping Leglock
- Leg Sweep

Melee Weapons (Sharp)

- Exploit
- Fast Attacks
- Hit & Run
- Vicious Attack
- Whirling Frenzy

DEADPOOL-BOT 2000

Art by Michael Shelfer & Fer Sifuentes-Sujo

RANK 5

KARMA —

HEALTH 240

DAMAGE REDUCTION -2

FOCUS 120

DAMAGE REDUCTION -2

SPEED
Run: 6
Climb: 3
Swim: 3
Jump: 3

INITIATIVE MODIFIER +4

BIOGRAPHY

Real Name: None
Height: 10'   **Weight:** 900 lbs.
Gender: Male
Eyes: White   **Hair:** None
Size: Big
Distinguishing Features: Giant clanky robot
Occupation: Adventurer
Origin: High Tech: Android
Teams: None
Base: Bagalia

HISTORY

When A.I.M. decided that nothing could possibly go wrong with creating an A.I. to train mercenaries, they evaluated a number of assassins, henchmen and hired guns. They even downloaded the thought patterns of a few of them—including Deadpool.

Deadpool's thought patterns corrupted the A.I., which started calling itself M.A.D.E.M. (Murderous Application Designed Exclusively for Mayhem). It created a number of hideous challenges to train—or slaughter—mercenaries. Among these creations was the Deadpool-Bot 2000.

PERSONALITY

This clattering, clunky robot believes itself to be Deadpool, and—like 90% of the comic creators in the world—it believes its own hype. It taunts opponents, cracks bad jokes and runs its mechanical mouth during battle... and pretty much all other times too.

ABILITIES

ABILITY SCORE	DEFENSE SCORE	NON-COMBAT CHECKS
7 MELEE	16	+8
4 AGILITY	13	+5
8 RESILIENCE	18	+8
4 VIGILANCE	14	+4
1 EGO	11	+1
1 LOGIC	11	+1

TRAITS & TAGS

TRAITS
- Abrasive
- Big
- Bloodthirsty
- Combat Expert
- Combat Reflexes
- **Connections:** Super Villains
- Fearless
- Tech Reliance ◈

TAGS
- A.I.
- Black Market Access
- Extreme Appearance
- Public Identity
- **Signature Weapon:** Giant swords

DAMAGE

MELEE	MARVEL dMarvel × 6 MULTIPLIER	+	7 ABILITY
AGILITY	MARVEL dMarvel × 6 MULTIPLIER	+	4 ABILITY
EGO	MARVEL dMarvel × 5 MULTIPLIER	+	1 ABILITY
LOGIC	MARVEL dMarvel × 5 MULTIPLIER	+	1 ABILITY

POWERS

BASIC ◈
- Accuracy 1
- Mighty 1
- Sturdy 2
- Uncanny 2
- Wisecracker

ELEMENTAL CONTROL (FIRE) ◈
- Elemental Burst (Fire)

MARTIAL ARTS ◈
- Chain Strikes
- Do This All Day
- Fast Strikes
- Grappling Technique

MELEE WEAPONS ◈
- Exploit
- Fast Attacks
- Hit & Run
- Vicious Attack
- Whirling Frenzy

SUPER-STRENGTH ◈
- Clobber
- Crushing Grip
- Ground-Shaking Stomp
- Smash

Note: If Deadpool-Bot 2000 faces more than four characters in the final battle, and they are not too battered, he gets to act twice in each round. He should roll twice for initiative.

DOOP

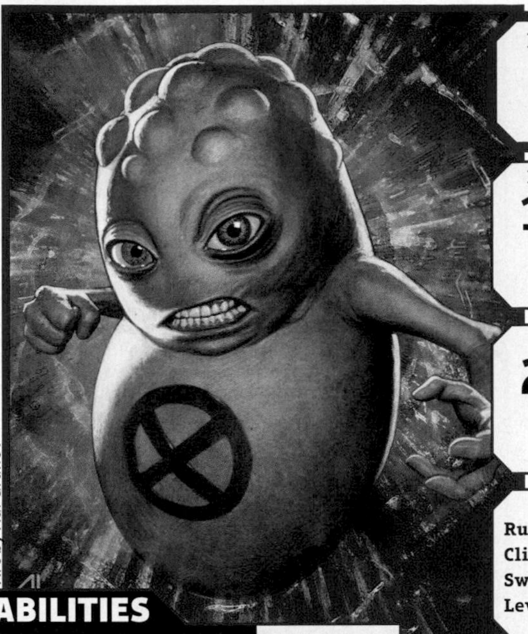

Art by Adi Granov

RANK	KARMA
6	—

HEALTH	DAMAGE REDUCTION
180	-2

FOCUS	DAMAGE REDUCTION
210	-2

SPEED
Run: 5
Climb: 3
Swim: 3
Levitation: 5

INITIATIVE MODIFIER +7E

ABILITIES

ABILITY	ABILITY SCORE	DEFENSE SCORE	NON-COMBAT CHECKS
MELEE	2	13	+2
AGILITY	5	16	+5
RESILIENCE	6	16	+6
VIGILANCE	7	17	+7
EGO	4	14	+4
LOGIC	6	16	+10

DAMAGE

	dMarvel × MULTIPLIER	+ ABILITY
MELEE	dMarvel × 6	+ 2
AGILITY	dMarvel × 6	+ 5
EGO	dMarvel × 6	+ 4
LOGIC	dMarvel × 10	+ 6

TRAITS & TAGS

Traits

- **Connections:** Outsiders
- Famous
- Font of Information
- Fresh Eyes
- Gearhead
- Situational Awareness
- Small
- Sneaky
- Stranger
- Weird

Tags

- Alien Heritage
- Extreme Appearance
- Mysterious
- Public Identity

BIOGRAPHY

Real Name: Unknown
Height: Varies, usually 3′
Weight: Varies **Gender:** Male
Eyes: Red **Hair:** None **Size:** Small
Distinguishing Features: Legless green creature resembling a large, fat pickle with arms
Occupation: Outsider
Origin: Alien: Marginalian
Teams: X-Statix
Base: Mobile

History

No one knows for sure where Doop came from, not even Doop. He grew up in the mysterious dimension of Marginalia, a place that exists outside of space and time, metaphorically in the margins of comic-book pages themselves.

Some say that Doop was the result of top-secret experiments performed by the U.S. military in the eighties. Others claim Doop spawned entirely from the imagination of an anonymous hospital orderly who scribbled the first known image of the creature in the margins of a screenplay written by film director Ingmar Bergman.

Whatever the truth may be, Doop spent his formative years believing that Ingmar Bergman was his creator. Out of respect for the director, Doop began practicing the art of filmmaking. Eventually, he lucked into a videography job with the private, for-profit X-Statix super-hero team.

Doop is the only member of the original X-Statix lineup still with the team. All the others either died or abandoned the group long ago, but Doop remains steadfast, always watching from the background, recording every movement.

When not with X-Statix, Doop mingles with mutants of all kinds. He once even served as a receptionist at the Jean Grey School for Higher Learning.

Personality

Doop has powers beyond comprehension, but he rarely uses them to their fullest extent. He does not want to make himself the subject of his own movies, preferring instead to let his teammates in X-Statix speak for themselves.

POWERS

Basic

- Brilliance 4
- Healing Factor
- Sturdy 2
- Uncanny 2

Omniversal Travel (Dimensional)

- Dimensional Portal
- Dimensional Travel
- Dimensional Travel Other
- Dimensional Travel Together

Power Control

- Clone Powers
- Copy Power

Resize

- Grow 2
- Shrink 2

Telekinesis

- Group Levitation
- Levitation

Telepathy

- Command
- Mental Shelter
- Telepathic Blast
- Telepathic Link

HIT-MONKEY

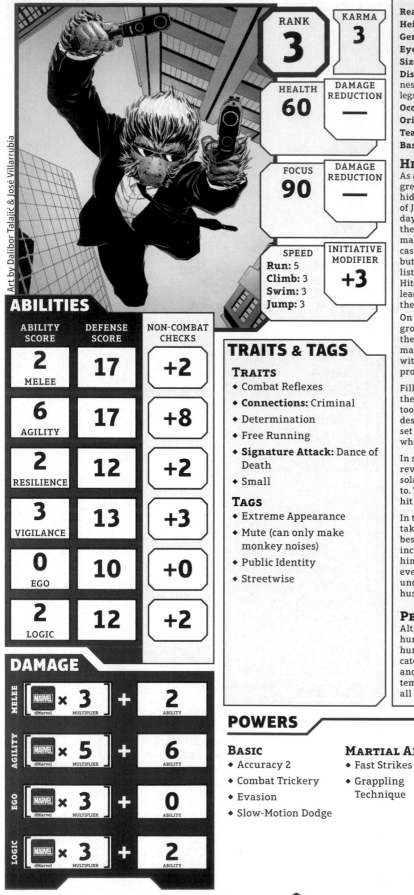

Art by Dalibor Talajić & José Villarrubia

RANK	KARMA
3	**3**

HEALTH	DAMAGE REDUCTION
60	—

FOCUS	DAMAGE REDUCTION
90	—

SPEED	INITIATIVE MODIFIER
Run: 5 **Climb:** 3 **Swim:** 3 **Jump:** 3	**+3**

ABILITIES

ABILITY SCORE	DEFENSE SCORE	NON-COMBAT CHECKS
2 MELEE	**17**	**+2**
6 AGILITY	**17**	**+8**
2 RESILIENCE	**12**	**+2**
3 VIGILANCE	**13**	**+3**
0 EGO	**10**	**+0**
2 LOGIC	**12**	**+2**

DAMAGE

	dMarvel	MULTIPLIER		ABILITY
MELEE	MARVEL	× 3	+	2
AGILITY	MARVEL	× 5	+	6
EGO	MARVEL	× 3	+	0
LOGIC	MARVEL	× 3	+	2

TRAITS & TAGS

TRAITS
- Combat Reflexes
- **Connections:** Criminal
- Determination
- Free Running
- **Signature Attack:** Dance of Death
- Small

TAGS
- Extreme Appearance
- Mute (can only make monkey noises)
- Public Identity
- Streetwise

POWERS

BASIC
- Accuracy 2
- Combat Trickery
- Evasion
- Slow-Motion Dodge

MARTIAL ARTS
- Fast Strikes
- Grappling Technique

RANGED WEAPONS
- Dance of Death
- Double Tap
- Slow-Motion Shoot-Dodge
- Snap Shooting
- Suppressive Fire
- Weapons Blazing

BIOGRAPHY

Real Name: None
Height: 2'5" **Weight:** 31 lbs.
Gender: Male
Eyes: Amber **Hair:** Gray
Size: Small
Distinguishing Features: Small Japanese macaque who often stands on two legs and wears a suit
Occupation: Assassin
Origin: Special Training
Teams: Mercs for Money, S.T.A.K.E.
Base: Mobile

HISTORY

As a young macaque, Hit-Monkey grew up among a tribe of his species hidden deep within the mountains of Japan. Life was peaceful until, one day, a dying hit man stumbled into the tribe's territory. Hit-Monkey demanded that the murderous man be cast back out into the snowy wastes, but the other macaques refused to listen. Determined to have his way, Hit-Monkey lashed out at the tribe's leader, injuring him. As punishment, the leader sent Hit-Monkey into exile.

On the same day that exile began, a group of hired mercenaries came to the mountainside, looking for the hit man. They slaughtered him—along with every one of the macaques protecting him.

Filled with rage upon discovering the fate of his tribe, Hit-Monkey took up the dead man's weapons and destroyed the mercenaries. He then set out for vengeance upon the men who'd hired those killers.

In short order, Hit-Monkey had his revenge, but it brought him little solace, as he had no home to return to. To keep on living, he became a hit man himself.

In the years since, Hit-Monkey has taken on and defeated some of the best mercenaries on the planet, including Deadpool. Many consider him the greatest contract killer to ever live. The upper echelons of the underworld utter his name only in hushed whispers.

PERSONALITY

Although Hit-Monkey understands human speech, he cannot speak any human language. He can communicate only with normal simian grunts and screeches. He has a hair-trigger temper, and in the heat of battle, he all but perpetually screams.

PALADIN

Art by Al Rio, Scott Koblish & Brad Anderson

RANK 3

KARMA 3

HEALTH 90

DAMAGE REDUCTION -1

FOCUS 60

DAMAGE REDUCTION —

SPEED
Run: 6
Climb: 3
Swim: 3
Jump: 3

INITIATIVE MODIFIER +2E

ABILITIES

ABILITY SCORE	DEFENSE SCORE	NON-COMBAT CHECKS
2 MELEE	12	+2
5 AGILITY	15	+7
3 RESILIENCE	13	+3
2 VIGILANCE	12	+2
3 EGO	13	+3
0 LOGIC	10	+0

DAMAGE

MELEE	MARVEL dMarvel × 3 MULTIPLIER	+	2 ABILITY	
AGILITY	MARVEL dMarvel × 5 MULTIPLIER	+	5 ABILITY	
EGO	MARVEL dMarvel × 3 MULTIPLIER	+	3 ABILITY	
LOGIC	MARVEL dMarvel × 3 MULTIPLIER	+	0 ABILITY	

TRAITS & TAGS

TRAITS
◆ Combat Expert
◆ Combat Reflexes
◆ **Connections:** Super Heroes
◆ Fearless
◆ Situational Awareness

TAGS
◆ Black Market Access
◆ Heroic
◆ Mysterious
◆ Secret Identity

BIOGRAPHY

Real Name: Unknown
Height: 6'2"   **Weight:** 225 lbs.
Gender: Male
Eyes: Brown   **Hair:** Brown
Size: Average
Distinguishing Features: None
Occupation: Adventurer
Origin: Unknown
Teams: Heroes for Hire, Villains for Hire
Base: Mobile

HISTORY
Paladin's past is a secret to everyone except maybe the man himself, and he isn't forthcoming with details. S.H.I.E.L.D.'s archives on Paladin date back only as far as a few years ago when, during a mission to capture the Purple Man, he fought with Daredevil. Although Paladin was already a moderately well-established mercenary by this point, no one knows for sure what jobs he had completed before facing off against the Man Without Fear.

Although Paladin ultimately failed to capture the Purple Man, his ability to hold his own against Daredevil made him famous overnight. Job offers came pouring in, from both super heroes and super villains.

For a while, Paladin sold his services exclusively to the highest bidder. Some days he was a hero, and other days he was a villain. He is one of the few people who can truthfully claim to have fought on both sides of the superhuman Civil War.

As the years drew on, though, Paladin's duplicitousness began to gnaw at his conscience. There was no single moment of reform and repentance, but slowly, he stopped accepting villainous jobs. These days, he works primarily as an independent hero for hire.

PERSONALITY
Ninety percent amoral mercenary and ten percent big-hearted softy, Paladin has a strangely charming aura. He's had a number of romantic relationships within the super-hero community, most notably with the Wasp. Even his enemies regard him as a gentleman and a consummate professional.

Paladin's need to make money exists in perpetual conflict with his conscience. He has, on several occasions, dropped well-paying assassination jobs at the last moment because he couldn't bear to kill his target.

POWERS

BASIC
◆ Accuracy 2
◆ **Iconic Weapon:** Stun gun [ranged weapon; deals electricity damage, stunning target on a Fantastic success]
◆ Slow-Motion Dodge
◆ Sturdy 1

MARTIAL ARTS
◆ Fast Strikes
◆ Leg Sweep

RANGED WEAPONS
◆ Double Tap
◆ Point-Blank Parry
◆ Slow-Motion Shoot-Dodge
◆ Snap Shooting
◆ Sniping
◆ Weapons Blazing

REN KIMURA

Art by Will Sliney & Veronica Gandini

RANK	KARMA
2	**2**

HEALTH	DAMAGE REDUCTION
60	—

FOCUS	DAMAGE REDUCTION
30	—

SPEED	INITIATIVE MODIFIER
Run: 5 Climb: 3 Swim: 3 Jump: 3	**+1**

ABILITIES

	ABILITY SCORE	DEFENSE SCORE	NON-COMBAT CHECKS
MELEE	3	13	+3
AGILITY	2	12	+2
RESILIENCE	2	12	+2
VIGILANCE	1	11	+1
EGO	2	12	+2
LOGIC	0	10	+0

DAMAGE

	dMarvel	MULTIPLIER	ABILITY
MELEE	MARVEL	× 3	+ 3
AGILITY	MARVEL	× 2	+ 2
EGO	MARVEL	× 2	+ 2
LOGIC	MARVEL	× 2	+ 0

BIOGRAPHY

Real Name: Ren Kimura
Height: 5'8"   **Weight:** 122 lbs.
Gender: Female
Eyes: Green   **Hair:** Black
Size: Average
Distinguishing Features: None
Occupation: Entertainer
Origin: Inhuman
Teams: Asgardians of the Galaxy, Fearless Defenders
Base: New York City

HISTORY

Growing up, Ren Kimura wanted to be a dancer. Unfortunately, her parents never approved of her aspirations or—for that matter—her homosexuality. She was forced to take up dancing (and dating) in secret, regularly sneaking away from home to spend long hours practicing at a local dance studio.

Because of this, Kimura was at the dance studio—not safe at home—when the Terrigen Bomb detonated over New York City. The Terrigen Mist activated the Inhuman lurking inside her genes, transforming her arms into twisted masses of metal wire. With effort, Kimura discovered that she could make the wires float through the air like dancing ribbons, able to slice distant targets to pieces.

That night, super villains invaded New York City, looking to kidnap the newly awakened Inhumans. Kimura would have fallen prey to them were it not for the intervention of the Fearless Defenders.

Kimura joined the Defenders and fell deeply in love with one of her new teammates: Annabelle Riggs. Even after the Defenders fell apart, Riggs and Kimura stuck together. They became part of the Asgardians of the Galaxy, and later, Riggs helped Kimura form her own dance studio. Although they've officially retired from the adventuring business, they remain ready to answer any call to action.

PERSONALITY

Despite their mutual affection, Riggs and Kimura have diametrically opposed personalities. Riggs is bookish, shy and more than a little awkward, while Kimura is as outgoing and charming as a person can be. She adores the stage and the spotlight.

TRAITS & TAGS

TRAITS
- Combat Reflexes
- Famous
- Glibness
- Presence
- Public Speaking

TAGS
- Heroic
- Inhuman Genes
- Public Identity

POWERS

BASIC
- Combat Trickery
- **Iconic Weapon:** Razor arms [hands act as melee weapons; +1 Melee damage multiplier]
- Inspiration

MELEE WEAPONS (SHARP)
- Fast Attacks
- Vicious Attack
- Whirling Frenzy

PLASTICITY
- Extended Reach 2

SHE-HULK (LYRA)

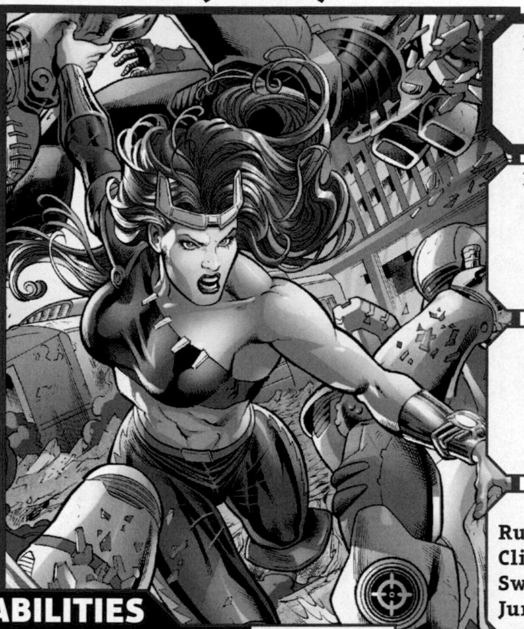

Art by Peter Vale, Robert Atkins, Nelson Pereira, Terry Pallot & Marte Gracia

RANK	KARMA
3	3

HEALTH	DAMAGE REDUCTION
90	-2

FOCUS	DAMAGE REDUCTION
90	—

SPEED	INITIATIVE MODIFIER
Run: 6 **Climb:** 3 **Swim:** 3 **Jump:** 18	+3

ABILITIES

ABILITY SCORE		DEFENSE SCORE	NON-COMBAT CHECKS
5	MELEE	14	+7
2	AGILITY	11	+2
3	RESILIENCE	13	+3
3	VIGILANCE	13	+3
1	EGO	11	+1
1	LOGIC	11	+1

DAMAGE

	dMarvel		MULTIPLIER		ABILITY
MELEE	MARVEL	×	5	+	5
AGILITY	MARVEL	×	3	+	2
EGO	MARVEL	×	3	+	1
LOGIC	MARVEL	×	3	+	1

TRAITS & TAGS

Traits
- Big
- **Connections:** Super Heroes
- Determination
- Fearless
- Iron Will
- Weird

Tags
- Black Market Access
- Extreme Appearance
- Green Door
- Heroic
- **Immunity:** Gamma Radiation
- Public Identity
- Radioactive

BIOGRAPHY

Real Name: Lyra
Height: 6'6" **Weight:** 220 lbs.
Gender: Female
Eyes: Green **Hair:** Red
Size: Big
Distinguishing Features: Green skin
Occupation: Adventurer
Origin: Weird Science: Gamma Mutate
Teams: A.R.M.O.R., Avengers Academy
Base: Mobile

History

On Earth-8009, massive environmental and military disasters long ago rendered the vast majority of humanity infertile. The survivors underwent experimental body modifications, granting them longer lives and incredible powers, and in the ensuing chaos, society stratified along strict gender lines, with the men of the world making perpetual war against the women.

In an attempt to gain the upper hand, one of the leaders of the female resistance—Thundra—stole some skin cells from the Hulk of Earth-616 and used his DNA to impregnate herself. Her daughter, Lyra, was the first person naturally born on the planet in decades.

When Lyra was just 16, her handlers sent her to Earth-616 so she could obtain fertile male DNA in much the same way her mother had. She was supposed to obtain cells from Norman Osborn, but once she saw how evil he was, she refused to complete her mission. Her handlers generously released her from her duties, allowing her to stay on Earth-616 and train with its heroes.

Over the years, Lyra has been tutored by many of Earth's greatest warriors, but she considers the original She-Hulk (Jennifer Walters) her number-one mentor. The pair are good friends, and Lyra sometimes uses the She-Hulk codename in honor of Walters.

Personality

When not in combat, Lyra has the personality of a normal, peppy teenage girl. In battle, she acts much more like a traditional stoic warrior. As opposed to most gamma mutates, Lyra's powers get weaker as she gets angrier. To keep herself in top form, she forces herself to roll with the punches, literally and figuratively.

POWERS

Basic
- Mighty 2
- Sturdy 2

Power Control
- Power Slider (Serenity)

Super-Strength
- Banging Heads
- Clobber
- Crushing Grip
- Ground-Shaking Stomp
- Jump 2
- Quick Toss
- Smash

WOLVERINE (LOGAN)

Art by R.B. Silva & Marte Gracia

RANK 4

KARMA 4

HEALTH 150

DAMAGE REDUCTION -1

FOCUS 150

DAMAGE REDUCTION -1

SPEED
Run: 5
Climb: 3
Swim: 3
Jump: 3

INITIATIVE MODIFIER +4E

BIOGRAPHY

Real Name: James Howlett
(a.k.a. Logan)

Height: 5'7"

Weight: 195 lbs.
(300 lbs. with adamantium)

Gender: Male

Eyes: Blue   **Hair:** Black

Size: Average

Distinguishing Features:
Retractable adamantium claws, muttonchops

Occupation: Military

Origin: High Tech: Cybernetics, Mutant

Teams: Avengers, Fantastic Four, X-Force, X-Men

Base: Krakoa, Summer House (the Blue Area of the Moon)

HISTORY

Born in Canada in the late 1800s, James Howlett wandered the world under the name Logan. At one point, the Weapon X program captured him and bonded adamantium metal to his entire skeleton, including his retractable claws; his mutant healing factor enabled him to survive the experience. He escaped, but with large gaps in his memory.

Logan later joined the X-Men and became a valued member of various X-teams. Over time, he recovered most of his memories. He was killed in recent years, but returned to life in time to help establish a new mutant nation on the island of Krakoa.

PERSONALITY

Logan can be cold-blooded and slow to trust others, but the restoration of his memory blunted those edges. He's still a no-nonsense man, but that's tempered with the wisdom age brings. After living as a loner for so long, he treasures his found family.

ABILITIES

ABILITY SCORE	DEFENSE SCORE	NON-COMBAT CHECKS
7 MELEE	17	+7
2 AGILITY	17	+2
5 RESILIENCE	15	+5
4 VIGILANCE	14	+4
1 EGO	11	+1
1 LOGIC	11	+1

TRAITS & TAGS

TRAITS
◆ Battle Ready
◆ Berserker
◆ Combat Expert
◆ Combat Reflexes
◆ **Connections:** Military
◆ Extraordinary Origin
◆ Situational Awareness
◆ Tech Reliance 🔲

TAGS
◆ Extreme Appearance
◆ **Enemy:** Sabretooth
◆ Heroic
◆ Hounded
◆ Krakoan
◆ Public Identity
◆ X-Gene

POWERS

BASIC
◆ Brawling
◆ Combat Trickery
◆ Healing Factor
◆ Heightened Senses 1
◆ **Iconic Weapon:** Adamantium Claws [+1 Melee damage multiplier; ignores 1 level of DR] 🔲
◆ Reinforced Skeleton 🔲
◆ Uncanny 1

MARTIAL ARTS
◆ Attack Stance
◆ Grappling Technique

MELEE WEAPONS (SHARP)
◆ Exploit
◆ Fast Attacks
◆ Focused Fury
◆ Furious Attacks
◆ Hit & Run
◆ Riposte
◆ Unstoppable Assault
◆ Vicious Attack
◆ Whirling Frenzy

DAMAGE

MELEE	dMarvel × 5 MULTIPLIER	+	7 ABILITY
AGILITY	dMarvel × 4 MULTIPLIER	+	2 ABILITY
EGO	dMarvel × 4 MULTIPLIER	+	1 ABILITY
LOGIC	dMarvel × 4 MULTIPLIER	+	1 ABILITY